Lynda Hykin

I0478661

Negotiation
for
Women

3 Simple strategies to finally take control –
of your money, your career and your life

Lynda Hykin

DEDICATION

To My Best Friend Judy
When I fell into the deepest, darkest hole of my life, you gently pointed me in the direction of the ladder.
Thank you my friend.

To My Grandson Noah
You are my inspiration and motivation – through your eyes I see how life was meant to be:
no limitations and endless possibilities.

And most of all, to My Daughter Jayme
Your strength and courage knows no boundaries. Every day I strive to try and capture that same unwavering spirit that you so naturally hold in your heart.

All of you helped to make this book a reality by believing in me, even when I didn't.

Thank you.

Lynda Hykin

CONTENTS

Lynda Hykin

PART TWO – MOMENTUM

TOP TEN REASONS

Lynda Hykin

PART THREE – MASTERY

Lynda Hykin

In the workforce and in society,

women have a valuable

contribution to make.

Learning to negotiate will help

them achieve equality in *all* areas of

their life.

Lynda Hykin

NOTE TO READERS

This publication contains the opinions and ideas of its author. It is intended to provide helpful and informative material on the subject addressed. The strategies outlined in this book may not be suitable for every individual, and are not guaranteed or warranted to produce any particular results.

This book is sold with the understanding that neither the author nor the publisher is engaged in rendering legal, financial, accounting or other professional advice or services. The reader should consult a competent professional before adopting any of the suggestions in this book or drawing inferences from it.

No warranty is made with respect to the accuracy or completeness of the information or referenced contained herein, and both the author and the publisher specifically disclaim any responsibility for any liability, loss or risk, personal or otherwise, which is incurred as a consequence, directly or indirectly, of the use and application of any of the contents of this book.

Lynda Hykin

ACKNOWLEDGMENTS

I thank T. Harv Eker author of Secrets of the Millionaire Mind, the book that blew the doors off my barriers.

Mr. James Malinchak, Big Money Speaker and TV's Secret Millionaire who taught me how to 'Do the Math' and 'Get stuff done fast'. The first I became an expert in, the second…well, I'm still working on that.

And of course, a woman I've never met (on my bucket list), yet changed my life unknowingly 13 years ago, Dr. Pat Heim, CEO of The Heim Group and author of Hardball for Women.

Lynda Hykin

.

PART ONE -

Motivation

You have to *really* want more to get more

PART TWO -

Momentum

Stand up, Speak Up and Ask for what you want

PART THREE -

Mastery

If you don't control your life, someone else will

Lynda Hykin

The Money Match-Maker Strategy System

The system I developed, teach and use in my own life, is called the "Money Match-Maker Strategy System". It has 3 parts that are inter-dependent. To get the most out of this book please read the 1st section before the 2nd, and the 2nd before the 3rd.

I actually created it from back to front; I learned the 3rd step first, then the 2nd. I knew these two steps worked but I felt like something was missing. I was getting what I asked for, but my bank account wasn't changing. I felt like there was a missing link. There was and I found it. It was the first step. Once I put the first step into place –wow! Everything came together; my career, my money, my bank account and my life!

Keep a notebook or journal for your thoughts, any 'aha's', and enlightening moments. I recommend this because I would love for you to share this book and although you may want to share my message, you may not want your deepest thoughts out there for others to see and read. (Of course, please feel free to buy them their own copy!)

I encourage everyone to recognize when other women don't go after what they want and to show them how because everyone can benefit from a mentor. If all you do is pass this book on to one person, it is a step in the right direction.

I know some of you just want to get to the 'good' stuff, and *then* you will go back and do the work and read the rest of it. Trust me, I have MANY books on my shelf, many reports in my email that 'I am going to get back to and do the work' … that are still waiting.

Funny thing is when I finally do get back to them I realize they have all kinds of information that I could have used to save myself an enormous amount of time, money and rework. Whether you read through once and then go back and complete the journal entries or do it as we go along, the choice is yours. To quote Oprah, "You always have the power".

Lynda Hykin

INTRODUCTION

The 1970's marked the beginning of my search for a life-altering, sky-is-the-limit, climb-to-the-top of-the-ladder career. This was the era that liberated women. We took control over our bodies and our lives. We *thought* we could have amazing careers, not just jobs. We *thought* we could climb the ladder to success all the way to the top right along side of the men! The doors were being held wide open for us to just walk in and take our place in the Working World.

By the time we reached the 80's, reality hit. Our first priority was still our family, our careers came second. We could 'play' at being "Career Women" but not at the expense of our family. Because of this dual role, by the 1990's, a lot of us suffered from what I like to call…
"Control freak-Martyr-itis".

It's a nasty disease that altered our thought process. It made us believe the only way to achieve both a personal life and a career was to
DO IT ALL! Be loving, caring and nurturing at home, and be the driven, tenacious bull dog at work. We had to be the best in both worlds.

To achieve this, we created…SUPERMOM! The fastest cook, cleaner, caretaker, corporate executive IN the world! We juggled babies and board meetings, T-ball and travel, read bedtime stories to our children, and remained 'womanly' for our man.

We had to fight the Glass Ceiling, the Sticky Floor, The Old Boys Club, and all the stereotypes that came with a woman wanting to make a place for herself in the Working World. We dove into this new game playing by the only rules we had to go by; the men's rules. We didn't have a set of our own. We suffered with the 'talk like a man, ride like a man and spit like a man' syndrome.

We thought we had to act like a man to succeed like a man. And how did the men and other women react? Let's just say "They were not amused!" In fact some Corporations spent thousands of dollars sending their women executives to "Be a Lady" School to make them 'tone it down'. They demanded women behave 'nicely' and never forget their true calling – "Be a good girl and get us coffee."

One enterprising woman, named Jean Holland, started a Company called 'Bully Broads'. Her Company charged $18,000 per person to 'reprogram' women executives to get them to act like a lady, like the men expected them to act. (By the way, her Company is STILL thriving today!)

The "b" word was thrown around like rice at a wedding. Women found themselves working twice as hard to get only half as far up the Corporate Ladder. They lost their core values. They could not be themselves, use their skills and talents in a way that was comfortable and effective for them – as women.

When it was all said and done; 30 and even 40 years later, most women STILL make less than men, we are promoted less, and earn deserved recognition less than men. Those top level positions are STILL out of our reach.

For whatever reasons I had at the time, I chose career paths of the *most* resistance. I spent mine in 'mostly male' environments (I know, what *was* I thinking?) I watched men get promotions, pay raises and perks. I saw how they negotiated to get career altering opportunities, yet never during all my various careers did I think to negotiate to get what I wanted.

Instead, I sat at break whining and complaining about how Lazy Larry actually got promoted, or how our supervisor got to drive a fancy company car when it was all the work *we* did that got him recognized. I knew how they got the promotions, the pay raises, and the perks… but I never once thought to do the same to get what I wanted.

I spent most of my time just trying to prove I was as good as the men, that I could do anything they could do, just as well or better… and then I waited to be recognized; for someone to come and tell me how good I was and that I was going to be rewarded for my efforts. IT NEVER HAPPENED!

But this did:

I worked on the production floor of a major manufacturing company. I became very good at Quality Control as part of my job. I assumed that sooner or later someone would recognize my abilities and skills and I would be promoted or get a chance to work on a project. Nope. What they *did* notice was the fact that my mechanical skills 'could use improvement'.

Every 6 months we had a performance review and every 6 months mine was the same; "You are really good at Quality Control, you have excellent communication skills, and you are great at training others, but you lack mechanical skills". Then the next 6 month action plan would include training and focus on where I needed to improve my 'mechanical aptitude'. 10 years later… that's right, 10 *years*, and I was still on the production floor, still trying to 'improve' my mechanical skills and still being passed over for opportunities to work on projects, pay level raises and promotions.

Then I worked with a different Line Leader. Once again, the same review produced the same comment; "You are great at Quality Control, but you really suck as a mechanic." Then he said something that changed my whole career path within the Company. He said, "I don't need 6 mechanics on my line, what do YOU want to do?" He actually asked me what I wanted!

It took less than 2 seconds to tell him. He helped me plan my next 6 months with the goal of working in the Quality Control Lab and *not* working on my mechanical skills. Soon an opening came up in the Raw

Material Lab, and I got the position. Within 18 *months,* I received 4 pay level raises. I travelled all over North America, met with suppliers on a global level, developed and implemented programs, worked as a team member making Corporate decisions, and had the opportunity to work on huge projects. I discovered capabilities and skills I never knew I had and I woke up every day loving my job.

Here's the really sad part:

I had the skill base to have taken that Lab position after just 3 years working for the Company. I might still be on the production floor, waiting for retirement to roll around if that person hadn't asked what I wanted. Plus, my new position gave me a NET weekly income of up to $1,100 per week (depending on the overtime/travel etc.)

The years on the production floor earned me a take home weekly income of $600. Do the math: I could have been earning up to an 'extra' $500 per week for 7 years but I didn't – because I didn't know I could!

End of story…

During my career with this same Manufacturing Company, I saw a video of a keynote speaker Dr. Pat Heim talking about gender differences, how men and women react differently to the same situation and why. When this video was over, I had a new career. She had such an impact on me that I made the decision right then and there that I was going to do what she was doing, help women understand these gender differences so they could be more effective at achieving their career goals. It would make their life in the workplace easier without always having to fight to get what they wanted.

I started researching these differences and spent the next 10 years collecting information, studying men and women and how they interacted with each other, specifically in the workforce. I discovered not only that the Glass Ceiling, the Sticky Floor, the Old Boys Club and all the typical stereotypes still existed, but that there was still a huge gap between what men and women earned; wage inequality was still thriving.

Want me to get your dander up, get the juices flowing and raise the blood pressure a little? (BTW, this is just the tip of the ice-burg!):

According to a 2008 report by Rosenzweig and Co., of the top 100 publicly traded companies in Canada:

- 74% are run at the highest level by men only
- 94.2% of the highest paid are men
- 97 of these top 100 companies have a Male CEO
- Only 31 women hold top level positions.
- Only 3 women hold the position of CEO

The number 1 ranked Company, the most profitable of all these 100... is the ONLY Company that also had multiple women in the top ranks, including a CFO and COO. (Coincidence??)

Before you think those stats are a little old, here is the Rozensweig Report 2 years later in 2010. (See page 189 for the 2013 report)

- 69% are run at the highest levels by men only - 5% increase of women
- 93.1% of the highest paid are men – 1.1% increase for women
- 35 women hold top officer jobs out of 547 positions - up by only 4 women
- 4 women hold the position of CEO – up by just 1 woman
- 6.9% of the most senior corporate offices are occupied by women, This was actually 7.2% in 2009
- Women represent 13% of these same Companies on the Board of Directors, but only 7% of Management Leadership

I kept digging to find out why. After all, laws were now in place to assure women Equal Rights, right?

I discovered a huge barrier for women – and it was one that was self inflicted. I discovered that most women don't ask for what they want.

Women don't negotiate. Women weren't asking for pay raises, promotions and recognition for their achievements. We were leaving *hundreds of thousands* of dollars behind over the course of our career simply because we weren't negotiating and asking for it!

It was almost impossible for me to get this information to sink into my brain and when it did I was not pleased with myself. I had been leaving all this money behind simply because I didn't negotiate. I didn't ask for opportunities and promotions or go after the recognition that I deserved for my job performance and successes.

That was a life changing moment for me. Then I made another decision. From that moment on I was going to always go after what I wanted. I was never again going to settle for less. I set out to ask for what I wanted.

The first opportunity came in a job interview. I was pumped! I wasn't going to take what they offered. I wanted $14/hr. and I was going after it. They offered $12/hr.
I took it.
No questions asked. No negotiating. No telling them that I wanted more. What happened? Where was my big plan to ask for what I wanted?

Enter the 'Aha' moment.

I didn't *have* a plan! I didn't know *how to ask*! I was not comfortable asking for more. I wanted to make the same money as the male co-worker working beside me, doing the same job. I wanted to go after the same opportunities to work on exciting and challenging projects when they came up. I wanted to plot my career so that promotions were available and I knew how to get them. but I didn't know how to do that.

Back to the researching…

I spent the next 3 years not just researching gender differences and wage inequality, but how to negotiate, how to ask for what I wanted.

I found nothing, or at least very little – for women. There were some high level Corporation multi-million dollar negotiation systems. Books for men – yes; books written for women by men – yes; books for women, written by women – not so much. Nothing for a woman like me who wanted to learn how to negotiate on an 'every day' level or who needed to learn from the beginning.

There are now some incredible books out there that tell stories of hugely successful women, some earning 6 figures and describing how they still have trouble asking for what they're worth. In fact I have read, learned and used some of the insights from these great books.

(A list of them is located at the back of this book. I highly recommend reading them all.)

But these women were *already* successful. They had fantastic careers, important positions, or were owners of their own incredibly successful business. But they weren't like me. They were who I aspired to *become*! I was at the bottom of the success totem pole, wanting to learn how to get to where they were. I couldn't relate to them.

I tried to find someone just like me – the lowly assistant – who had visions of being the millionaire entrepreneur, the brilliant and savvy business woman. I was starting from scratch and needed to learn – from scratch. I couldn't find anyone or any techniques or strategies to get me where they already were, where I *wanted* to go.

I decided to create my own system. I took everything I had learned from my research, studying men and women, gender differences in the workplace, the wage inequality that still exists and my own experiences and put a system together. Then I tested it - over and over again. It worked! I had other women use it, and they were successful. It was simple, powerful, and it worked!

That's why I wrote this book. This is the 'system'. This book will walk you through simple steps so you can discover why we don't, why we should, and how to negotiate; as a woman - from the beginning.

This next decade will offer women opportunities like never before. Our leadership style, knowledge and skills are gathering in a huge talent pool of women that Corporations are just now beginning to realize is what is needed to catapult their Company into the future. Corporations need to recognize the value of the style of leadership that women bring to the table and how the Y Generation will more willingly engage in this leadership as opposed to the current hierarchy, whose time has come.

The Working World needs to acknowledge how important it is to retain talented women and their expertise, and they need to recognize the simple fact that there will be a desperate need to replenish the fast-depleting skill base. Not only does the Working World need to know this, but *women* need to know this. With this knowledge and the practiced skill of negotiation, women can narrow the wage gap and truly reach their full potential – in all areas of their life.

If I can do this **any**-one can because I am just like you. I now ask for what I want all the time, in all kinds of situations, not just in my business, but my personal life, in my community or in a strange new environment. I recognize opportunities to make my life better and I go after them. I am now **in control**. The more I ask for what I want, the more confident I become. And when I am successful, the more my bank account increases!

The stories in this book are real – because they are my stories. These stories are what happened to me and how I lost out and then I figured out, how to become that other woman – the successful one, the one with the career I wanted, the income I wanted, and the knowledge and skill to earn, hold and grow my wealth. To get what I am worth.

I want to bring awareness to girls and women everywhere; to help them find their way to enlightenment and liberation, to succeed in the path they have always known was theirs, and to have the financial freedom to live the life they choose.

I wrote this book to offer you a chance to finally understand yourself, your relationship with money and to understand why you don't ask for what you want, why you should and most of all, how to use simple, yet powerful negotiating techniques to ask for what you want – and get it.

Turn the page; it may change your life…

Lynda Hykin

*"If money be not
thy Servant*

*it will be
thy Master"*

- Francis Bacon

Lynda Hykin

CHAPTER 1

MONEY AND ME

AKA

OIL AND WATER

My relationship with money has never been shall we say, a profitable one. In fact, we didn't seem to get along well together at all. The majority of my life was spent living "paycheck to paycheck". Most of the time, there wasn't enough. The few times that I did receive large amounts of money, it didn't take long to spend it all and return to being broke and unhappy. In fact I NEVER saved money.

If I could find a way to have something **now** rather than have to save for it, I would; through loans, credit cards, borrowing from friends or store credit. That was so much easier than having to save for something I wanted. How boring is that.

Sometimes I think I invented the phrase, "Immediate gratification". I wanted everything now, and became an expert at justifying all the purchases and investments I made, to convince myself I made the right choices at the time, with the information I had. Oh, who am I kidding? I made those purchases and choices just because I WANTED them.

My budget was simple: If I made $2,000 I spent $2,000. If I paid all my bills (which didn't happen often or on time) and there was money left over I spent it, whether I needed something or not. If I had to choose between something I wanted and a bill – the 'something' usually won. Apparently, my goal was to have $0 in the bank at all times.

I hated living this way but it had become my 'way of life' and quite frankly the only life I knew. I would dream about having thousands of dollars in my bank account; then I would never worry about feeding my family – which I sometimes couldn't do. I wanted money in the bank so I would have a safe place to live, which I sometimes didn't have.

Yet I would constantly get into financial trouble. When I finally dug myself out of a bad financial situation (which was frequently) I would make a promise to myself that, "If I get out of this mess, I will NEVER let it happen again!" But it did, over and over again, for most of my life.

This was my philosophy:
Life was to be lived and enjoyed, and in order to do that I had to spend! Why hoard money away for a rainy day; who wanted it to rain? Besides, I was going to be young forever!

As it turns out, I wasn't young forever. Suddenly, or so it seemed, I was a Mom and then a Grandma, and still didn't have one cent in the bank. Imagine, 40 years of working, and zero dollars to my name. The only plan I could think of was hoping that the government pension would still be there when I became eligible. Even that was still ten years away.

This began to terrify me. Here I was, supposed to be getting ready to enjoy my life after work – and I was still trying to figure out how to pay my rent.

Then a life changing moment.

Someone questioned me about my belief about money. What did I think about money and what did I see and hear when I was younger? My first recollection about what I saw and heard about money as a child **immediately** popped into my head. A whole scene began to unfold:

When I was little I was a 'Daddy's girl'. He was my idol and my hero and I hung on every word he said. I adored him and in my eyes, he could do no wrong. One day when I was about 7 years old, my Dad and I were outside with a neighbor and one of my friends. My friend and I decided we wanted to get some candy at the store. I asked my Dad for a dime. He said he didn't have any money, he was broke. What? Of course he had money!

I kept bugging him. Finally he put his hand in his pocket and pulled out some change (and dramatically, the lining of his pocket). Among those few coins in his hand was a dime. As I reached to take the dime, my Dad looked at me incredulously and said, "Do you mean to tell me that you would take my very last dime? This is all I have."

The implication to me was clear and what I heard, in my child's mind was, "How greedy can you be?" I knew I had disappointed my Dad. I had hurt his feelings and all because I wanted a dime. I must be greedy. The worst part was I still wanted that dime, which I knew made me a very bad person. Imagine wanting to take someone's last dime just for myself. What I didn't know until years later was that Dad really was broke, and that it **was** most likely his last dime during that period, which just validated the fact that I was greedy and a bad person for wanting to take his money.

That single incident set the foundation for my financial future. If I had money I was greedy. I must give it all away so no-one will think I am a bad person. Other people should have money, not me. Giving my money away to others will make them like me and I will be a good girl. My Dad certainly never meant for me to feel bad, he was most likely just frustrated because he couldn't give me what I wanted. But as a child I believed my Dad knew *everything* so he must have been right to 'show me' I was greedy.

There were plenty of other things and situations that occurred and they all reinforced the fact that I should live without money because it was wrong to want it. "What do you think I am, made of money?"(you`re greedy) Money doesn't grow on trees, you know! (you`re greedy) Again and again 'you're greedy for wanting something' was what I heard. They all piled up in my sub-conscious mind and stayed with me, and I unknowingly created my financial life around this belief.

Once I started working and making my own money, I felt free! I could buy whatever I wanted, when I wanted. It was MY money, and I could do whatever I wanted with it. I wasn't taking it away from someone else so I wasn't being greedy. I moved away from home to attend college, and never looked back. I thought I was in control (silly me). Spend, spend, spend! Life was good – until I ran out of money. Luck was on my side though because it introduced me to a fabulous 'money tree' called credit card! Spend, spend and spend again!

Did you know that you can buy a car using your student loan money? I know, because I did it. Of course, then I had to leave college and get a job to pay for the car- but that just meant being able to spend more money.

I quickly racked up thousands of dollars in credit card debt, using the cards for food at the high end deli shops because I didn't have enough cash to buy it in the regular grocery store. I was paying $7/lb for chicken – and that was back in the '70's. Ouch. I moved whenever I couldn't pay rent. I borrowed money from my parents, and never paid them back. I ran out of money 'trees' and did what I became an expert at doing – burying my head (and problems) in the sand. If I ignored them long enough, and out-ran them, I figured I would be okay. (I wasn't).

Sometimes it worked – most of the time it didn't. My credit rating was proof. Then I would clean up my act … until the next session of being irresponsible (referred to as "I can do what I want`") came along.

From time to time, I had nice things; a house, car, beautiful furniture, but I always managed to give them away, sell them dirt cheap (because I needed money), lose or have them taken away. I used the excuse many times over that I liked a 'clean slate' and liked to start over. Mostly it meant I had forced myself into a situation where I HAD to start over.

I married a man who had the same philosophy as me, no surprise there, right? I actually became the 'responsible' one in the family – well sort of. I knew we should pay our bills, and tried to make sure we did, but we still enjoyed spending and living way beyond our means. Needless to say, the money and the marriage didn't last.

This time I was not only once again on my own, with the same attitude about money, but I now had a daughter that I was responsible for. I knew I had to make sure my daughter didn't live the financial way I did and I tried to teach her *not* to be like me.

I explained to her how to save (because I'd read it in books and magazines), showed her how money came in and went out with play money, as if it were a game. She was a genius at knowing how much 20% off something was, or what 'buy one, get one free' worked out to for each item. She was also very savvy at spending my money, but very cautious spending her own.

My words however, were never as potent at teaching her as what she saw me do and how we lived – I was always broke - or had money for a very short time, immediately spent it and then broke again. I would tell her it was good to save, to not spend more than you make and then I would just keep on doing what I had always done.

My daughter did have more willpower than me. She would be tenacious enough that if she really wanted something she would save for it – buy it – but then slide back to the way she grew up, the way I had *really* taught her.

My 2nd marriage came when I was earning a great income with a Manufacturing Company. We were both working and we should have been laughing all the way to the bank. We weren't. He let me take control of the finances (silly man). When I met him, he had a credit card, a vehicle that was paid for and good credit. We bought a little house with a mortgage payment of only $500 per month. We had an income of up to $6,000 per month. We were broke every week.

A short few years later, we (I) lost the credit card because we (I) didn't make the payments. We bought a car and a truck but somehow couldn't make the payments. We (I) lost the car and the truck. We separated.

I was back to being on my own, with my daughter – doing what I had always done. I took a severance package from my job (the most money I ever had at any one time), bought a bigger house that had a rental income and created a plan for saving, even going as far as handing the money over to a financial planner. I went back to College and afterward, opened up a retail store. Then I began to spend my new financial plan.

Within two years, I had to sell my car, my house and declare bankruptcy. A very long struggle over many years, low paying jobs, bouncing around from place to place, but always faithful to the only way of financial life I knew.

I received another sum of money when my Mom passed away through an inheritance. I bought a rental building, opened a retail store (again) – and within 3 years went broke, closed the store, lost the inventory I had remaining and back to square one.

This time however, I was *really* scared. I was now over 50 years old. I had nothing, zero dollars. I was not young anymore. It was harder and harder to find a decent paying job that wanted someone who may collect on sick benefits in the next few years. But I didn`t know what to do differently. I didn't know how to fix it. So, back to doing what I always did – move.

This time, I sold everything I owned (not new), left my family and friends (not new) and moved over 2,000 miles away to a place I`d never been, with only 2 friends that I had just recently reconnected with after 35 years, no job, and no idea what the hell I was going to do (VERY new).

I actually had my first ever (and only) panic attack when the plane was about to land. What had I done?? I must be crazy! How will I live? Where will I live? What about money??And even worse; I couldn`t go back, because there was nothing to go back to! The only reason I didn't hop on a plane and go back as soon as the plane landed was the simple fact that there were no more flights out until the next morning.

The long drive to my friend's home was a blessing and helped to calm me down. I relaxed by telling myself that I would treat this like a vacation. My friends were gracious enough to open their home to me for a couple of weeks (which actually turned into a month). I am now and forever grateful to Bob and Joanne for all their love, support, and allowing me to be their long-term house guest.

I gave myself the two weeks to find a job. On the 14th day, I had a job. (That was cutting it a little close, don't you think?)

A month from the time I arrived, I moved into my very own apartment.

I made a commitment to myself that I would NEVER go back to the old ways again. I was done with living that way. I actually did pretty well – for awhile.

Then it was back to the old comfy me.

Welcome home – to Broke and Un-Happyville. (Sigh)

End of story

Finally, after living this way for *over 40 years*, the "AHA" moment came. When that person questioned my beliefs about money and that story from my childhood *immediately* popped into my head, I knew I was onto to something special. Questioning what I believed about money made me finally realize that my entire relationship with money was based on what I saw and heard *as a child*. The fact was, my Dad NEVER said I was greedy or a bad person for wanting money. It was the perception of what I thought I heard because I was only a child.

This discovery changed my entire life! This meant that everything I knew, everything I believed about money was based on a *child's* belief. I now had to make room for new grown-up thoughts and beliefs. All the old garbage information that I would be deleting or rejecting, I now had to replace with better, more prosperous thoughts. I was now open to a whole new way of financial learning.

Research! First I began to check out people that were already successful, that were already financially free, living the life I would like to live. They obviously knew something I didn't. I started to follow their systems, their programs and methods, and started doing what they did. It worked.

The next thing I did was simplify my life. Simplifying makes things so much easier and I definitely want my life to be easier. The fancy 2 bedroom, 2 bath plus den condo that I rented was now gone. In its place - a one bedroom suite, which immediately saved me $350.00 every month. Then more simplifying. The one bedroom suite, gone. In its place – a great roommate, and only one bill to pay; rent. This was the turning point in my bank account. I now had over $1,200.00 every month that I could put toward 'Debt Zero'.

Did I prefer my fancy condo or living alone? Not when I saw all that money left over! I got to sleep at night. My bills were paid. There was no chance of the gas or electricity being shut off because that was all taken care of.

Little by little I followed the steps and slowly I started to crawl out from under the ``debt rock``. This wasn't instantaneous. Remember, it took me fifty years to create my life, so it was going to take a little while to undo what I had done and create a new life. Slowly, good habits began to replace the old. I developed an awareness of triggers – those impulses and devil-on-one-shoulder/angel-on-the-other conversations.

I began to notice how often I would have a conversation with myself, trying to justify a purchase. I felt that 'rush' of money/spend whenever I got paid. My old thought was – money! What can I buy? The new me was – money! What can I pay off?

Did the 'old me' want to go back to the way it used to be? All the time. The old me did not like this new stuff at all. But I recognized that as a good sign. I must be doing something right, because it was different from anything I had ever done before and what I had done before didn't exactly work out too well.

In my old world I thought like this:

Discipline = denial;

Saving money =denial;

Paying Bills in full on time =denial.

Of course, that just made it harder. When you think you are denying yourself something, that's all you can think about. It becomes your focus, which sets you up for giving in, which then makes you feel guilty, which then makes you say, 'forget it, I can't do this' which leads straight back to the comfort zone of the past.

I used to actually get a rush when I decided I didn't want to do the 'good thing' and that it was easier just to do what I always did. Did I slip? Absolutely. Many times. But each time there was more awareness, more conversations that the new me won. And I was beginning to actually have money – and feel GOOD about it!

Hitting bottom (several times) just made me even more determined. Awareness and recognition came faster and faster. Good decisions were made more and more often. Soon good choices and decisions were thought of – first.

Darren Hardy, publisher of Success Magazine, has a great way of putting this into perspective:

When you are faced with choices, choose the one you don't want to do. The one you want to do is most likely the one you've always done, which brought you to where you are. If you don't like where you are…. don't do what you've always done!

Lynda Hykin

JOURNAL ENTRY 1

Answer the following questions:

1. What is your belief about money? (is money good/bad/irrelevant to you?)

2. What did you hear and see when you were growing up when it came to money?

3. What were some favorite phrases that your parents or other adults used? For example – "Money doesn't grow on trees", "We can't afford that".

4. Were you from a wealthy family, one that struggled, or middle class? How did you feel when you associated with others from a different financial class?

5. Was one parent a saver, the other a spender?

6. Who controlled the money in your house?

7. Did both parents work outside the home? Did you grow up in a single parent situation?

8. Is there one incident that you can immediately recollect about money and how it made you feel?

9. Did that incident have an impact on your current belief about money? Why?

10. Is that belief even true?

Lynda Hykin

VOLUNTARY EXERCISES

Whether you are a spender like me or totally the opposite – a saver, you may benefit from the following exercises. We need to be a balance of spender/saver to enjoy life the most. Too much of either one is not good. It's developing a respect for money, and a respect for ourselves that evolves when there is balance. Enjoy!

Answer the following questions:

1. What are you doing with your money now that you don't want to do anymore?
2. What aren't you doing with your money now that you do want to do?
3. Do you know what your money comfort zone is?

Exercise:

Write down your dream income (no limits!!) on the back of a card, or separate piece of paper. On the other side write down you current annual income. Now raise it by $10,000 thinking as if this is going to be your new income, starting next month. Keep raising it by $10,000 until you start to feel uncomfortable. Don't stop, keep going until it no longer excites you; it is making you agitated or frustrated and is totally unbelievable for you.. Now go back and circle the income that **first**

started making you feel uncomfortable. This is the outer limit of your comfort zone.

How close was the number you circled to your dream income? Often, women have actually gone past their ***dream*** income before they started to feel uncomfortable. This is because they have a low self worth value when it comes to income. (More on this later.) Use this number as your beginning point. This will be your starting income goal, you will want to refer to this later. (By the end of the book however, it may totally change!)

More questions:

1. Do you spend less than you make?

2. Do you pay yourself first before paying any other bills?

3. Do you have a long term savings plan that is *currently* active?

4. Are you spending more than 70% of your net income on necessities?

5. Do you give a portion of your income back as gratitude for all you do have - consistently?

6. Do you save any of your income for short term savings (car, vacation, etc)?

7. Do you have enough money in the bank to cover 6 months worth of bills should you suddenly lose your income or have an emergency (car/house repair), family emergency?

8. Do you have credit card debt? How much? Loans? How much? How much is your mortgage/rent? Is it taking up most of your income?

9. If you lost your income/job – how would you pay your bills, where would money come from?

Exercise:

1. Add up EVERY bill for this month

Do not round down. Do not think, "If I'm careful it would only be this much". Record EXACTLY what you owe THIS month.

2. Get an envelope.

Every time you buy something ask for a receipt - for EVERYTHING; coffee, chocolate bar, bus ticket, everything you buy. If they won't supply a receipt then carry around a little notepad and write what you spent in it. It's much more powerful to have the receipt though, so try.

If today is the 13th, don't wait until the 1st. Go from the 13th to the 12th of the next month. (Remember, I AM the guru at being broke and unhappy – I know all the tricks, especially procrastination!).   Don't think about what you are spending – spend as usual. At the end of the month sort them and then add them up; how much on coffees/entertainment/gas/clothing/etc. This will show you where you are spending your money. It was quite the eye-opener for me! A dollar here or there doesn't matter – unless they total $50 or $60 and they did!

3. Pay yourself first

Open a new account, preferably one with *HIGH banking fees* for withdrawal. The plan is not to take anything out of this account, so penalties for withdrawal will make you think before you do. If you set aside money for yourself first before paying anything else, you are going to make sure there is enough left over to pay your bills, which means your bills can't exceed your income minus what you pay yourself. This money goes into a long term savings plan of your choice.

The principle amount is NEVER touched! It must accumulate interest. The interest is then used only for investments and creating passive income. The principle is *never* touched. Make it come out automatically to go into your bank account through payroll deduction. This will curb your desire to find an excuse not to do it one month. Coming directly out of your pay also makes the deductions smaller because you are depositing it more than once per month so the 'hit' doesn't 'hurt' as much. Set it up on the day you get paid. Begin to research long term savings plan options so you become knowledgeable in where to earn the best rate for your money. The goal is to put 10% of your income into this account. Right now, that may be impossible – but put **something** in. It's the habit that counts, not the amount.

4. Simplify

I don't like the word down-size. It's negative and can imply failure. I prefer simplify. Simplifying means easier. If you can make your life easier, that's a good thing. You don't have to go to the lengths that I did, by moving into a roommate situation, but think about where you can make changes to simplify. Only 50% of your income should be spent on necessities- housing/food/medical. If you are spending more than 50%, you need to simplify. Mortgages are based on 25-30% of your income. The rest of the 50% pays utilities, food, clothing, transportation and whatever you deem to be a necessity. My necessities are probably much different than yours. It has to relate to you and your family.

You may need a car but do you *really* need the Ferrari? You live alone, so do you *really* need to rent the 2 bedroom, 2 bath waterfront condo *in case* out-of-town company comes? That was why I had mine. The extra money you're saving on rent/mortgage/car payments/etc. now goes toward paying down your debt.

Unless you have money like the Jones' – you can't live in debt trying to keep up with them. Here's a secret; nobody really cares about where you live or what you drive – except you. They're busy trying to live their own life. Besides, the Jones' could be up to their eyeballs in debt trying to keep up with *you*! If that $5 latte every morning is a must-have, then the money for it has to come from somewhere, so choose your treats. Personally, I don't like cooking for just me so I like to eat out. This money comes out of my grocery money, and no, I don't increase my grocery money to include this!

5. Make a list of all debt

Make a list (no sugar coating) of *all* credit-cards, loans, mortgage, any creditors like in-store credit, everybody. Include those creditors that are harassing you on the phone, the ones that have put a red mark on your credit rating. Take the *smallest* debt and put 10% of your income on this bill. Pay the minimum on all the rest. You start with the smallest because you will pay it off the fastest and you will get a sense of accomplishment/success sooner. As soon as that bill is paid off, grab a BIG red marker and cross it out or make happy faces all over the final payment, whatever you want.

Celebrate! NO, not by spending the 'now free' money that you don't have to use on that debt anymore – sheesh! Take the next smallest debt, put 10% of your income PLUS the money that is now free from the other debt and apply. Continue to **destroy** your debt at an amazing speed!

By the way, you can negotiate with your creditors to reduce interest or remove it completely, have them take their bad rating off your credit report and more. You can also have someone like a Credit Counseling Service do this for you, depending on your situation. This is research for you. Look for non-profit companies; some profit-making companies charge astronomical fees to do this!

When all debt is gone, this becomes your short term saving. You may use this for things like furthering your education, seminars, workshops, vacations, a newer car or special events.
BUT ONLY AFTER THE DEBT IS GONE!

6. Did you just get a raise at work?

Congratulations! Whatever is was, don't let it melt into your income. Instead, use it to pay down more of your debt, then put it in your savings/investment account. Sorry Charlie, it is not a call to upgrade as long as you have debt.

7.   Start a change jar

Put all your loose change in it. Put up to 10% of your income in it. When it is full, take it to your favorite charity or community organization and give it to them. Giving is the fastest way of receiving more and it feels so good! After all, you are probably pretty depressed with having to save all this money, and pay off bills and stuff. Might as well make yourself or better yet, someone else feel good.

8.   **Reward Time!**

That's right! You get to spend!

10% of your income goes into this account. Hurray! Listen, you cannot deprive yourself completely for too long. It will only work for a little while, and then you will (if you're anything like me) splurge – feel guilty – say 'screw it' – and splurge again. Then *poof!* Just like poor Cinderella – you're back to living in a pumpkin!

The fun part is you must spend this money every month on *you*, not a bill. Play and Pamper at will. **One small note** – do not just contribute to this account and not the others. Other than necessities, all other accounts are created, treated and contributed to *equally*. (Keep in mind I am the what-not-to-do-guru!)

So how many of you noticed there is 10% not accounted for? (Just checking.)

9.   **Sleep-at-night**

The last 10%. This goes into an account that is never touched, except in an emergency. (A BIG sale at Macy's is NOT an emergency – or that pair of shoes that are 50% off). This is your life-saving, I-can-sleep-at-night-knowing-it's-there money. Should an accident happen; the water pipes burst, loss of income etc. you know you have at least 6 months of income in the bank.

When I asked myself, 'if something happened to my family, do I have enough money to fly home to be there' – the answer was 'no'. I got that money saved up pretty fast. It is never touched. It is not used to visit on a vacation. It is 'emergency' travel money.

Whether you are a spender or saver, a giver or hoarder, everyone can benefit by becoming more aware of how you spend, when you spend and how much you spend.

I found that if I carried cash, it was gone much quicker than if I had to use my debit card. With cash, I wouldn't think twice about grabbing a coffee at Tim Horton's or a treat at the convenience store, but if I had to put $1.50 on my debit? I thought twice about it. I felt silly using my debit for anything under $5.

I didn't realize how much I actually spent on those under $5 things, until I stopped carrying cash; same with the credit card. It stays at home. It also cuts down on impulse buying. Another funny thing happened. Because I wasn't grabbing a burger, an ice cream cone, a piece of pizza, or a donut with that coffee…. I lost weight! Who knew that saving money helps you lose weight!

The hardest part for me was the money in the Savings Accounts. It would taunt me and tease me, "Hey Lynda, look, I'm here. Helloo, it's Money! Yoo-hoo, come and get me!" It's still a struggle not to spend it, but I feel so good knowing it's there and I don't *need* to spend it. My necessities are covered and I have spending money.

We have to create new money habits. Do at least 2 or 3 of the action steps that you just went through. If you can do them all, that's even better, but rather than fail and give up, start with the 2 or 3 that really hit home for you. Do them for 90 days. Realistically, that is only 6 pay-checks for most people. Certainly you can do it for that short a period, right? Some of you might be saying, I can't do that… I have too many bills.

It doesn't matter if you do this with 10% of your income or $1.00. The point of the exercise is to just start. It's creating a new, better habit that counts. The more you do it, the easier it becomes, until you don't even have to think about it. As your income increases and your debt decreases, add more to each. You will be amazed at how fast you reach the 10% mark.

Doing this will have a definite impact on you… and your bank account.

Here is a little secret that I found happened to me when I applied these exercises and only those that have read all the way through to here get to be in on it! I lost weight and began to love exercise. I had more energy. I looked great. My head was held up a little higher and my self-esteem got a huge boost.

More on this later…

CHAPTER 2

DISCOVER YOUR 'WHY'

Perhaps the information in the previous chapter meant little to you. Unlike me, you are an excellent saver, have great credit and are financially responsible. You may be doing all those steps already. Congratulations if you are.

You may be thinking, "What does all this have to do with the first strategy that states: "You have to *really* want more to get more?" Maybe you are wondering what does any of this have to do with negotiating.

The simple answer is, you need to know where your money is going. You need to know how much you have and how much you really want, where you would like to add more, how you would like to change your lifestyle (bigger house, better car, more vacations) and how you are going to pay for it. You need to get control of your money first, so that when you are earning more, you have the habits already in place and working in order to manage more.

If you are not making the kind of money you dream of making, (remember the comfort zone for those who did the exercises?) something is blocking you, stopping you from getting what you *really* want.

It could be your 'why'.

What motivates you? We are either motivated by fear or motivated by possibility. We need emotion behind either one of these, fear or possibility, in order to change. No emotion – no change.

Here's a Question:

3 frogs are sitting on a lily pad and one decides to jump off. How many are left on the lily pad?

If you said 2, congratulations! You were THIS close to being right! The right answer is................ 3.

Why? Because the frog only *decided* to jump............ he didn't actually do it.

We have all sat around from time to time, wondering what it would be like to win the lottery, or perhaps thought about all the things we are going to do when we retire. Maybe we've wished to have a different life style than the one we currently wake up to each morning. We call these daydreams, wishful thinking and fantasies. They're fun to think about, but we don't REALLY expect them to happen. And we don't do anything to MAKE them happen. We may buy a lottery ticket, or surf the web, looking for exotic places in far-away lands to build our dream home or Bed and Breakfast on. We may glance at the want ads, looking for a new job. But that's as far as we take it.

What if you're like the frog? What if you decide you are going to DO something, make a change or live differently than you do now? Making that decision means you are actually setting a goal and making a commitment to yourself. Think about this; I'll give you 5 seconds.

If you could only do one thing for the rest of your life, and I could guarantee that you would not fail, what would you do?

Time's up!

Did you know exactly what that would be? Did you use the entire 5 seconds to think about it? Maybe still don't know? The frog knew. He wanted to jump off that lily pad. Yet all he did was make a decision to jump, he didn't actually do it. He's still sitting on that lily pad. "Yes sir, I'm going to jump. Yep, I'm going in!", but there's no splash.

We can set all the goals we want, make thousands of decisions to do something but if we just sit back on our 'lily pad' and wait for UPS to deliver, nothing is going to happen. Until we get off our 'lily pad' and start doing something about it ... NOTHING is going to change!

This is the part where we actually have to work to achieve our goal, to fulfill those decisions that we made. And this is the part where most people turn decisions back into daydreams and wishful thinking.
"I don't have time, I'm too busy, when the kids are gone, I don't have the education, the money", blah, blah, blah.
My question now to you is.............. are you like the frog?

How important is it to you to get to the next level, to be a millionaire if that is your goal? **Why** do you want to be a millionaire?

One of my goals is to have a beautiful 5,000 sq. ft. home in Costa Rica. When I first asked myself why I wanted my dream home (and the money to pay for it and maintain it), the immediate answer that came to mind was, "So I can show all my friends and family that I AM successful, that my 'scatter-brained' ideas worked!" As soon as I said it, I knew that wasn't an answer that would make having my home a joy for me, for several reasons:

- My family and friends, in fact no-one, should determine what I do, scatterbrained or otherwise
- I shouldn't have to prove anything to any-one
- Do my family and friends *really* care where or how I live?
- My home should bring me joy and not be used for self-validation

All that really meant was my self-esteem was low and needed a boost. It meant I didn't think I was successful, I didn't think I deserved to have it. I had to re-think my 'why'.

Now, the only reason I want my beautiful house in Costa Rica, is because – it's beautiful! I want to be surrounded by beauty. I want to feel happiness, peace and joy in my own home. Is that a strong enough, long-lasting enough reason for me to do everything I can to make it happen? For me, it is.

Your 'why' will be something different for you. Perhaps it's because you never went to College, and you want to make sure there is money for your children so you don't have to worry about whether they have the best chances that you can give them. Perhaps you don't want to see your parents live in poverty in their retirement years and want to be able to help them live comfortably. Perhaps you want to make sure your family is looked after should anything happen to you. Find your 'why'. I actually got stuck here. It really took me a long time to figure this out. I had to do some digging and soul searching to find it. Let me see if I can help you with that.

Why do you want more money? It seems like a simple question (um - so I can buy more things!) But is that REALLY why you want more? What does the extra money mean to you? What will it provide for you? What freedom can it give you? What impact can you make with more income? Who can you help with more money? If the only reason why was to have more things, you would have all the things you want already, right? So, it seems like it doesn't quite work that way.

How does it work?

Your why must be profound. It will be something that the pain of not having it is greater than the 'comfort' of being able to live without it. If it is just something that you would *like* to have, you will not do what's necessary to achieve it. If you have a strong enough why, you walk through the fear and never quit until you achieve it.

Think of it as a 'Cause'. How much harder do people work at something if they truly believe in the Cause? They are more determined to succeed, more committed to results, more willing to be a vocal and an action-taking advocate for the Cause.

If my 'why' is strong enough, if my reason is so that I can live in a tropical paradise surrounded by beauty, clean air and warm sunshine, I will do whatever it takes to get it and never quit until it's achieved.

Is it hard? Sure… but only if you make it hard.

A business associate recently gave a speech to my Money Masters Meet-up Group that I organized. After her speech, we had a Q and A and I asked her what helped her make the decision to go from 'dabbling in her business' to making 6 figures in just over 18 months.

Her answer went off like a gunshot in my brain – "I just decided that failure was not an option". So simple.

A few weeks later while at Houston Airport I was sitting in front of a T-shirt kiosk. Bored, I went over to browse. There was a T-shirt with "Failure is not an option" emblazoned on the front.
I bought it.
I wear it when I run and I feel like quitting. I wear it when I'm feeling like things are too hard. I wear it when I don't want to push myself out of my comfort zone. I wear it when I want to just run away.
(I should have bought a bunch of them, because this one is getting a lot of use!)

What is your 'why'? Write it down. Carry it around with you on an index card. Put it on your computer, your bathroom mirror, in your car. Your mind will do EVERYTHING to make your why a reality. It has to. That's its job. You tell it that this is the 'new reality'. Your mind will HAVE to find a way to make it happen.

My dream home is a reality. It is just a matter of time, just waiting for the perfect time for me to own it. I really don't care about the how. There is absolutely no doubt in my mind that I will have this. And every time I negotiate for something I want, it brings me closer to having it. The money, promotions and recognition I get moves me forward to achieving my why – my home.

I'm okay with getting uncomfortable and negotiating for that raise because the outcome is SO worth it! If not negotiating means I don't get it? You can be darn sure I'm asking for what I want. It's not just the $2/per hour I'm asking for. It's for my dream home!

Lynda Hykin

Create your why.

The mind will now take it from here, thank you.

JOURNAL ENTRY 2

1. List and number everything that you *seriously* want in your life, that would cause you to go through being uncomfortable in order to achieve it? Keep them short and simple. I want a Mercedes, a vacation home in the Alps, etc.

2. Start with number 1, is it more or less important than number 2? If you could only have one or the other, which would you choose? If number one is more important, go to number 3. Is number 1 more important than number 3?

3. Keep doing this until you've gone through the list. If number 1 is more important than all the rest, put it on a 2nd piece of paper as number 1 and it is taken out of the list.

4. If, as you go through the list number 6 becomes more important than number 1, then number 6 becomes the one you judge the remainder of the list.

5. Continue until you have your top 3 These become your 'why'.

If you feel that 3 may be overwhelming to work on at the same time, just pick your first one. Instinct is the best guide here.

Answer these questions:

- What are you willing to give up in order to achieve your why? (TV, chips…)

- What do you need to start doing?

- What do you need to stop doing?

- What do you need to learn?

These are now to be used as 'negotiating' tools. These are what will make being uncomfortable worthwhile, when you are in there asking for what you want, for what you deserve. They will bolster your will when you really want to turn around and run! When you ask for that raise, that promotion, it's because of your 'why'.

It is incredibly powerful to take your 'why' into a room with you when you negotiate. If you don't think you deserve something for yourself, that's one thing, (and we will change this attitude later) but if your child's education is on the line? – *that* can turn meek and mild into mother bears. You are no longer just asking for something for no reason – you have a BIG reason!

Simple, powerful … and it works!

(Read The Passion Test by Janet and Chris Attwood to get the full benefits of this exercise)

CHAPTER 3

DO THE MATH

From now on I want you to repeat your new mantra. Every time you come up with a choice; whether it's a purchase, a job, or a sale, repeat your new mantra and whip out your trusty calculator. (No excuses, there is one on your phone!)

These three words are your new mantra:

"DO THE MATH".

From now on, simply do the math. If the numbers don't work, they don't work and you can't change how they add up.   A great 'virtual' mentor of mine, James Malinchak of TV's Secret Millionaire taught me this when I attended one of his bootcamps for Speakers. He is a multi-millionaire, so I listen because I figure he knows what he's talking about.

Check this out. If you are a business owner, entrepreneur, sales person on commission, or aspire to have your own business, do the math. If your goal is to make a $1,000,000.00 this is all you need to know:

How many units at what price?   If you are in sales, how many units do you have to sell at what price to earn what you want to earn?

1	Unit(s)	at	$ 1,000,000.00
10		at	$ 100,000.00
100		at	$ 10,000.00
1000		at	$ 1,000.00
10,000		at	$ 100.00
100,000		at	$ 10.00

Or another way to look at it:

If you sell a service, such as consulting, or accounting, and you want to earn $1,000,000.00:

1	service	at	$1,000,000.00
10		at	$ 100,000.00
34		at	$ 30,000.00
200		at	$ 5,000.00
400		at	$ 2,500.00
2000		at	$ 500.00

It's easier when you see the numbers. This is realistic, and should get you motivated. You can actually *see* how to get to a million dollars.

Now, do you *really* want to get there? Do you really want to do the work that is required to get those numbers? How many can see yourself selling, making, distributing or whatever your job is, to do the math? You have to make changes in your life, in what you are doing right now. What you are doing right now is not working, or at least not working the way you want it to.

Here is a great motivator and negotiating strategy:

If you are making $16.00 per hour at your current job, ask if you can reduce your base salary to $14.00 per hour and earn a 3% commission on everything you sell, or a bonus for sales over $ X. Earning $16.00 per hour will never make you $1,000,000.00. Commission however is unlimited; the more you sell, the more you make.

Did I notice someone feeling a little uncomfortable with that?

Let's say you are an employee, working for a Company, and your goal is to earn $400,000 a year. Based on 52 weeks, at 8 hours a day, 5 days a week, with two weeks off for vacation, this means you are working for $200.00 per hour. Here is the way the average person thinks when doing the math:

"$200 per hour? I could never make that much an hour!" So instead, we do this:

$ 400,000 = $200/hr

$ 200,000 = $100/hr

$100,000 = $ 50/hr I can do that!

Now instead of your goal being $400,000 you've *reduced* it until you are comfortable. Did you *really* want that $400,000? Instead of getting excited about making $400,000 a year, you are now excited about earning $50per hour which is going to make you just $100,000.

And your 'why' just went out the window.

Your brain is an excellent piece of equipment. Give it a question, and it is the brain's job to find an answer. It will keep searching until it comes up with a solution to the problem you have given it. Rather than settle for less, ask your mind how you can make $400,000 per year, or $200 per hour. Let it find a solution. It will search everything that comes into your life; everything that you see, hear, and think, perhaps yanking out old files that you buried; a plan or an idea that you long-ago filed away. It has to find a solution.

Decide what you want. Then do YOUR math. If the current numbers don't work, they don't work. You can't manipulate them to make them work. If your 'why' is $400,000 start looking for solutions to get $400,000. Take your 'why' and do the math. Then be open to receiving 'the how' because it will show up.

Opportunities and solutions will start presenting themselves to you. No matter how you do the math, $12/hr does not equal $400,000/yr. Making $10/hr flipping burgers will not see you earning $400,000/year; owning your own burger place might. The solutions to your 'why' are out there, just waiting for you to connect.

You know what your 'why' is. Now you know how to 'do the math' to get it. Is anybody wondering yet what does this have to do with negotiation? I'll tell you – everything.

You have to ask for what you want and you are sometimes going to negotiate so you can get you closer ... to what you want! Knowing what it is you want and the numbers you need to get it will encourage you during a negotiation.

Remember to take your 'why' with you, especially when you negotiate, when you ask for something. Why do you want this raise, that promotion or that new client? Will this new job, client, promotion bring me closer to my 'why'?

"How will getting a $2/hr raise get me closer to what I want?" It will take forever to earn $400,000 if I only get an extra $2 per hour!

Here is a scenario * that may put it into perspective:

Two prospective employees, a man and a woman, graduate from the same University with the same marks and degree. There are two Jr. Buyer positions available in ABC Company. Both candidates are equally qualified and have the same skills.

The two interviews proceed like this:

The interviewer tells the woman candidate, "Congratulations! You have been chosen for the position AND we are going to offer you $1,000 more than the starting rate, so your salary will be $30,000." She thinks, wow, not only did I get the job, but they gave me $1,000 more than the starting rate! I am on that ladder to the top! She thanks the interviewer and accepts the position and salary.

Next door the male candidate is being offered the same position. Again, the offer is for $30,000. The male candidate says "With all due respect, I believe with my education, skills and performance record I would have been at the top of your salary range, based on the research that I have done among other companies." The interviewer states that they never start anyone out at the top of the salary range, however they will increase the offer to $33,000. The male candidate says, "What if I accept $36,000 to start, with the provision that my salary is reviewed in 6 months and adjusted based on my successful performance to $38,000?

They finally settle. The male candidate will receive a starting salary of $35,000 and after one year will be re-evaluated based on performance and if successful, will receive $37,000.

Both candidates meet outside in the hall and congratulate each other. The female proudly boasts that not only did she get the job, but she is getting more money than the starting rate. The male says great, me too!

He asked, she didn't.

Why go through all that just for only $5,000 more, right? It doesn't seem like such a biggie.

But wait, there's more ...

He puts that $5,000 extra in an account that earns 3% interest. You both continue to earn average increases of say 3%. But because his base salary was already $5,000 higher at the beginning, his 3% will be more than hers. If he takes the difference between what she accepted at the beginning and what he is earning and put it into that same account, by the time retirement rolls around at 65, he would have earned over **$800,000** – simply because he asked for more just **that one time!**

Ahem ... Mantra please ... (do the math!)

Most women are leaving that kind of money behind on the table simply because they don't ask for it. Can you use an extra million dollars or more? Would that help out your 'why'?

There is money just waiting for us to pick up, but we are not comfortable talking about it, and definitely not comfortable asking for it.

We need to overcome this aversion to talking about what we want for ourselves.

Money itself is just paper. It has no value. If I gave you a million dollars, told you to shove it under your bed, and never spend any of it, what is it worth? Nothing, it's just a bunch of paper collecting dust (and under my bed that's a lot of dust!) It's only worth the value we give it; it's what you **do** with the money that matters, that can make all the difference.

Everyone has a purpose in life, whether or not they know consciously what that is. We are here to make some kind of impact. How much more of an impact could you make, if you earned what you were *really* worth, if your career was something you truly loved, and if you were passionate about what you do?

If you REALLY want to make more money, make a bigger impact, make a better life for your family, make your community a better place to live, find out what is stopping you.

Get motivated – to want more!

*(similar to scenario from the book Ask for it by Linda Babcock and Sara Laschever)

JOURNAL ENTRY 3

You don't have to share this with anyone so be honest. After all, it's really hard to lie to yourself. You know deep down when you are.

Right now, you may not know how you're going to get it done, you just need to know that you have decided that you will. That's all you need for now.

Do your math. What is your number? Remember in Chapter One, you found your comfort zone number? How far above that do you think you could REALLY go?

Decide from your 'why' list what you want. Then work back-word from that to figure out what you need to achieve your goals. For example, I want to have $100,000 in the bank. How much do I need to earn to pay all my expenses, and save $100,000?

Do you know, right now, something, somebody, or some way to help you achieve the math you've just calculated or at least start you on that path?

Although all roads may lead to your goals, it will never be a straight line. There will be curves, hills, mountains, and detours. Sometimes the road even gets blown up. These are what make it a journey, what makes it and you feel alive! Just always remember that if you are doing something that is not moving you toward your goal (your why), ask yourself what do you need:

- To do – to get you on back on that path
- To stop doing - that is preventing you from moving forward

Find out what you don't know that will help to get what you want (like how to negotiate for what you want for instance?) See? I told you this wasn't hard! Is anyone out there starting to feel excited yet?

Lynda Hykin

"Do what you fear

and the death of fear

is certain"

- Anthony Robbins

Lynda Hykin

PART 2

MOMENTUM

The Genie will grant your wish -

But you have to ASK for what you want.

(So why don't we?)

Lynda Hykin

INTRODUCTION

Joanne Lipman, the former deputy managing editor of The Wall Street Journal and editor-in-chief of Portfolio magazine said that during her years as an editor, "Many, many men have come through my door asking for a raise or demanding a promotion. Guess how many women have ever asked me for a promotion? I'll tell you. Exactly… zero."

My 3 main reasons for doing what I do, and sharing what I've experienced and learned are these:

1. Only 1% of all the wealth in the world is owned by women

2. In July 2010 Canada ranked 4th in the World for having the LARGEST wage gap. In 2009, we ranked 5th … which means we are going in the WRONG direction! We do not want to be the winner on this list.

3. According to the 2011 Women's Leadership Development survey 71% of global organizations do not have a clearly defined strategy or philosophy to develop women for leadership.

In case you need a little more incentive to want to change things or a little extra push to change yourself, here are a few other reasons it is crucial to bring change to the Working World:

- The majority of the poor in Canada are female. According to a Statistics Canada Report on women, one in five Canadian women lives in a low-income situation. Those at highest risk of poverty are:

  - Female

  - Unattached seniors

  - Young unattached women

  - Female lone parents

  - Women with disabilities

  - Aboriginal women

  - Visible minority women

- More and more women hold down two or three jobs to put together a full-time wage. In the last 10 years, the number of women holding multiple jobs has grown by 45%, while the number of men holding multiple jobs has risen by only 4%.

- Wage inequity follows women for life. Since the Canada Pension Plan is based on an individual's earning history, many women retire into poverty. The average CPP benefit in 2011 (cannot find updated stats) paid to women was $285 per month; for men it was $410 per month.

- **Women own about 40% of all businesses in the** U.S. but receive only 2.3 percent of the available equity capital needed for growth.

- Men are expected to earn 13 percent more than women during their first year of full-time work and 32 percent more at their career peak.

This is only the tip of the iceberg and these change daily – and not in a good way. It would be a complete encyclopedia series if I put all the stats that I have collected and researched in this book, so I just pulled a few to make my point. We know we should ask for what we want. We need to know why we don't.

MY TOP TEN REASONS

WHY WOMEN DON'T NEGOTIATE

1. Fear

2. What YOU believe you're Worth

3. Gender Differences

4. Good Girl Syndrome

5. Low Expectations – Self Discrimination

6. Achievements

7. Work-Life Balance

8. The Word 'No'

9. Taking Risks

10. Lack of role Model/Mentor

I believe these are the most common reasons why women don't ask for what they want. If we are going to eliminate the wage gap, and start attaining the careers we were destined to have, we must knock down our self-imposed barriers.

Lynda Hykin

1. FEAR

There is a beautiful park that I ran through every morning when I was living in Richmond BC. On one run the first week of May, I saw a Mama duck with a whole whack of babies waddling down to the pond. Honestly, there must have been 15 or 20 babies! When they got to the pond, Mama went right into the water. One brave little one followed right behind. The rest stayed at the top and squawked, but didn't venture any further. Mama ignored them. I wanted to get a closer look and as I approached the babies, an interesting thing happened. About half the babies saw me coming, and waddled as fast as they could, down into the water and to the safety of Mama. But a few stayed still or hopped around, sensing danger but not knowing what to do about it.

The next day; same Mama, same babies (I'm guessing). This time when Mama went into the water she was followed by most of the babies. Still a few hung back until I approached. Then they too went in. Only one or two STILL didn't follow.

It made me think about fear. The babies were afraid to follow Mama into the water. But when a bigger fear came along (me), they chose to jump into the water, to brave the 1st fear. The 2nd time, it was easier for them, they weren't as afraid because they had already done it once. It didn't take long before they were all waddling down all by themselves without a 2nd thought. The fear was gone.

Women have a fear about negotiating, about asking for something for ourselves. Just hearing the word 'negotiate' terrifies us. Surgery without anesthetic would be better than having to negotiate! Whenever I mention the 'negotiate' word to women, the body language speaks loud and clear. If the woman is standing, she backs up, or makes an excuse to move away. I've even had some women walk away! If they are sitting, the arms cross, the legs cross, and they sit as far back in their chairs as they can get.

We picture ultimatums; getting so angry that we break down and cry, or up and quit right then and there; perhaps we may say something we *really* wish we hadn't! Most likely we've all seen men 'performing' the TV version of the negotiation ritual: Men pounding on the table, eyes and veins bulging, yelling and screaming, stomping out of the room.

Why on earth would we want to put ourselves through all that just to get a couple of extra dollars, right?

Apart from the images we have, there are more reasons we fear asking for what we want:

- We are afraid of jeopardizing the working relationship. Women establish some kind of working relationship with coworkers, colleagues and their boss. We do not want to damage or put a strain on these relationships, just to get something for ourselves. Plus, there is the, "What if he gets mad at me for even asking?" "I'll seem so ungrateful for what I already have." "If I ask, and he says no, it will be so hard to regain his trust and work comfortably together again".

- We worry that we will be labeled with the 'B' (bitch) word. Nice girls don't ask. If we ask for something for ourselves, we will appear pushy, self-serving, and greedy.

- We fear losing our job, or not getting it in the first place. "There are others that are willing to take the job for the salary they are offering." "I really want this job. I'll figure out the salary later." We have the misconception that once we have the job, once we demonstrate what we can do, we will be recognized for all our hard work and the value we bring, and then we will get compensated. This rarely happens. In some cases, women will actually turn down the job, rather than negotiate for salary, hours or other compensation.

We have to lose the fear. If you know exactly what you want, and why you want it, you are half way there. Do you remember the first time you rode a bike? Did you eventually get over the fear? Do you enjoy the feeling of accomplishment when you tackle something you've never done before?

Did you know that 85% of HR interviewers EXPECT salary to be negotiated? Did you know that men negotiate their salary 4 times more often than women? Does knowing this now make it a little easier? That it is okay to do?

Plan to get Uncomfortable.

You have to put on the tight-fitting shoes and get a little UN-comfortable. The first time you negotiate, you will be very uncomfortable, like ANY thing we do that is not considered 'normal' to us.

It is a new habit. Did you know that it only takes 31 days to create a new habit? Considering the reward at the end of those 31 days, isn't it worth being uncomfortable for just a little while? Each time we do it, it gets easier and the fear gets less and less. Each time you try, you will gain more confidence.

Movie Stars, Singers, Performers and many other successful people still get butterflies, still feel uncomfortable before they perform. The difference is, they do it anyway. Like the little ducklings, the fear for you *now* is that you *know* you are leaving thousands and thousands of dollars behind, unless you speak up and ask for it. What is your bigger fear; asking for what is already there, waiting for you – or leaving behind all that money and what it could mean for you?

Finally, the biggest fear is that women are afraid they are not worth more. Wages, perks and compensation have always been dictated to us. We are told what our skills, experience and capabilities are worth by the employer. This appears as 'what we are worth'. We just assume we are making what is fair, what everyone else is making, what we are worth.

Which leads me to Number 2 ...

Lynda Hykin

1. WHAT YOU BELIEVE YOU'RE WORTH

When I was looking for reasonably priced suites in Vancouver (as if there IS such a thing), I found one suite at $850 and two at $750 all in the same area. I put the ads on my phone so I had the addresses and went to check them out. I checked out the $850 ad first. After viewing it, I explained to the lady that I had two other places to look at before I made a decision, and frankly, they were $100 cheaper than hers and in the same area. She looked at me with that 'sure they are' look. I pulled up the ads on my phone and showed her. She offered me her suite for $750.

That easy.

I knew what the suite was worth. What does this have to do with knowing what you are worth? Everything. Keep reading.

I spend a lot of time working with women in the Administrative field, so I pulled some information on 'competitive' wages. These are taken from the HRDC website.

- Administrative Officer for a College - $21.00 per hour for a 40 hour work week

- Office Manager – same duties as above - $22.00 per hour

- Assistant- same duties - $18.00 per hour

I chose these particular ads because they were exceptional. Most Administrative positions offer between $12.00 and $14.00. (by 2012 standards.) The thing is, the skills and qualifications were the same for all the positions, basically the same duties.

Which hourly rate would you prefer; the $22.00 per hour or the $12.00 per hour for doing basically the same work? If there are positions out there that offer a higher wage for your skills, why would you settle for less?

It's because we assume that what they are offering is all that we can get, that they are being fair, that jobs and positions are individually priced and our skills must adjust to their price. We are looking at this the wrong way. Instead of the job dictating what we will get, we need to start telling them what we are worth. We need to show them that our skills are worth what we are asking for, regardless of what they expect to pay or what they advertised.

Wow! I'm really pushing it here right? As if you would EVER go in to an interview or to your boss and tell them what you expect to receive for your qualifications and skills. Well that's EXACTLY what I want you to do… and with confidence!

HOWEVER, before we can ask for what we want, we need to know what our skills are worth - to us, the market, and our boss.

Find out.

No-one is going to come to us with a list of the best jobs, the best wages and the highest price you can get for your skills. We have to go looking for it. Whether it's the internet, coworkers, networking and talking to others in the same field, or just hanging out at various functions, find out.

Here are some questions to research the answers to:

- What are others making in the same field as you?

- What is the median for your job title?

- Where in the range do you place your skill level – beginner/intermediate/expert?

- What are other Companies in a similar field paying for your experience and skills?

- Are you taking course after seminar after workshop and not being given an opportunity to use what you've learned? Perhaps you are using it, but not getting paid for it. Does your boss even *know* you took the seminar, workshop or course? Does he know all that you do?

- Do you get compensation or at least recognized for all the 'extras' that you do, over and above your job description?

- Do you consistently 'volunteer' your services without mention of compensation?

- If there is a salary range, where do you put yourself on the scale? Do you set yourself up for the low end, even though the high end was what attracted you to the position in the first place?

- Have you ever found an ad with a Company that had a reputation as a terrific Company to work for, and the job was very interesting, but you wouldn't apply because they advertised a salary that was lower (or higher) than what you wanted?

I am guilty of many of the above. It hurts to think about all those missed opportunities just because I wouldn't think to negotiate. What if I had stated my salary expectation based on what I knew my skills were worth with one of those Companies? What is the worst that could have happened? What if I had shown them why I was the best candidate and worth the extra few dollars? They may have hired me! But I'll never know, because I didn't ask.

We have to stop assuming; assuming they won't pay what we want, assuming we don't have the skills, assuming if we asked for too much, we will take ourselves out of the game.

If you don't know what your skills are worth, get tested, ask others in your field, check out advertisements for similar positions, even if you are not actively seeking another job.

My salary expectations rose significantly after I had been tested by a couple Temp Agencies. I found out that my skill level was certifiable (no-not "I was certifiable") my skills were! I was actually very proficient in certain areas, and could claim 'expert' status. This pushed me to start looking for jobs in a whole new dollar range. I would never have known if I hadn't been tested.

The higher the value *you* place on your skills, experience, and qualifications, the more you are going to be perceived to be worth. This results in you and your skills being in demand more than the 'average' candidate, and therefore you can negotiate a much more satisfactory package. (the word package here is a clue of things to come…)

Once you know your value, and what you can bring to the Company, or the employer, you are in the driver's seat. More than qualified? We'll talk more about this later, but know that those 'extra' skills and values can be used as bargaining chips, because you will be able to use them to describe why you're the best, and how those extra skills are going to help your boss reach the next level of *his* career, increase *his* income, make him look good to *his* boss, or save him thousands of dollars, and why he should pay for those extras.

It's all in the value. How you value your skills and abilities is how you value yourself. How you value yourself is how you create your self-esteem and self-confidence. The perception of 'value' is that if it is expensive, it's worth more, you get more for your dollar, better quality and so you should pay more. What seems more valuable – a purse from Walmart, or one from Louis Vuitton? If we view ourselves, our skills and abilities as being a valuable commodity, we will be perceived as being worth more. Employers want value. They want the best. They also want to get it for the least. They may offer a lower salary even if they are aware that your skills are worth more. (Can't blame a guy for trying right?) They also know most women won't question it.

When you KNOW you're good, it shows. The way you walk, the way you interact with others and the way you do your job. I constantly hear myself thinking (or sometimes saying out loud), 'Damn, I'm good!' and I mean it. It's a boost to my self esteem. When you're good at something, you strive to get better and better at it. You learn new skills, take on more, you seek out bigger, better and more challenging opportunities and you learn to get paid for that.

Guess what? That means you are now worth more! And the cycle begins!

I call it ...

The Circle of Success

Use the Circle of Success no matter what you are asking for:

- A new vehicle

- Loan

- Mortgage

- Rent

- Suppliers

- Clients

- Phone Services

- Daycare

Anything can be negotiated when you know what the value is, what others are paying and what the market is allowing. Apply and repeat this cycle as often as you wish, for the rest of your life! You can negotiate for anything when you know what YOUR value is!

Sometimes going in circles – is a *good* thing!

3. GENDER DIFFERENCES

This was the catalyst for me and what began my journey toward my purpose in life. This is what started my quest, my life-long passion, and this is what I have studied and researched the most. I conduct seminars just on this topic alone, as well as my negotiation strategies. It's incredibly fascinating and instead of being a barrier, I use it as an extremely powerful tool to help me when I negotiate. I could write a book on this subject all by itself (hmm).

Psychologists believe children by the age of 2 can distinguish the gender of adults. By 6 years old, they can recognize, understand and think of items in terms of 'gender'; toolbox as male, ironing board as female. For you gen-y-ers, that's an old fashioned tool used along with an iron for removing wrinkles from clothes. We were taught we could be, do or have anything we wanted when we were little... as long as we stayed within our 'gender' stereo types. Even today, gender differences are still promoted ... even from the most enlightened parents!

My daughter came to visit with her 10 month old son. Playing with him she nonchalantly said, "I'm so glad I had a boy so I can be rough and tough with him". When I asked her –with the hairs standing up on my arms and my heart beating wildly - why she couldn't do that if he had been a girl she replied, "I don't know, you just think that you're supposed to be gentle with girls". This from my own daughter!

And the stereotypes persist:

Girls in pink, boys in blue. I recently went by a "Babies R Us" window display and sure enough, one side was decked out all in pretty pinks with dolls and teddy bears. The other side was decked out in blues with soccer balls, airplanes, and footballs.

- Girls play indoor games, boys play outdoor sports.

- Boys are taught not to cry, to 'suck it up and walk it off'.

- Girls are taught to nurture, to make *other* people feel better; their needs are to come second after others.

When is the last time you saw a child 'win' when they were playing with dolls? Unless they were transformers, smashing and annihilating evil beings, or UFC wrestling figurines, you don't win at a game of dolls. Most 'girl' games do not involve a winner and loser. They promote 'getting along', helping others and playing nicely together.

The object of the typical male game is to win. The winner controls. The winner is the best. Sorry, but no little boy really feels happy when his team loses, 'although they played their best'. The goal was to win. What do girls do when they win, and the other team loses? They commiserate with the other team and try to make them feel better! They 'secretly' enjoy the win, but they don't 'rub it in'.

This difference continues through-out school, into life and into the workplace. Women want to make everybody happy. Women know if there is a winner, then someone loses and they worry about the feelings of the one who lost. Men promote their win. They make sure everyone knows what they did, how they did it, and what they expect because of it. Even if we don't realize it, we still encourage stereotypes, although we may *think* we're teaching the opposite.

Here are some questions to think about (and this is meant for the average home, there are always exceptions):

- Who drives when the family goes together in the car?
- Who does the indoor chores like dust, vacuum, dishes etc?
- Who does the outdoor chores like cutting the lawn, shoveling snow, cleaning eaves?
- Who is most likely encouraged at an early age to earn extra money?
- Who drives the 2nd hand car?
- Who would move the family for their career?
- Does the woman in the family have a 'part-time' or 'gives her something to do' job?
- Whose job is considered more important?
- Do you pay your son to wash the car, but not pay your daughter for doing dishes?
- Who calls in to work and stays home when a child is sick?
- What feels more uncomfortable – a girl playing with a group of boys, or a boy playing with a group of girls?
- Do your children participate in 'gender' activities; boys take karate, girls take ballet?
- How many families do you know where the boy takes ballet, and the girl plays hockey?

Perhaps those may have come out somewhat even for your family. Try this:

Very quickly without thinking, visualize the following people in these roles:

Lynda Hykin

Biker on a Harley

Nurse

Garbage Collector

Massage Therapist

Wrestler

Receptionist

Construction Worker

Plumber

Were they male? Female? Both?

Stereotyping is still alive and stubbornly refuses to die of old age. There are now laws to protect women from discrimination, and certain types of stereotyping - The introduction of the Equal Employment Organization, Affirmative Action, and discrimination laws have all helped to shape public awareness. But it doesn't mean it still doesn't happen.

During an interview for a Manufacturing Company I was asked, "Who will look after your kids while you're working 12 hours shifts?" Apparently he noticed on my resume that I was a single mom. This question is illegal to ask!

Although my resume clearly showed that I had seldom worked in the Administrative Field, the interviewer also made sure I 'understood' that I could not wear dresses or skirts, that I would be working on a production line and not in an office, that I would get dirty, that I may break a nail, and would that interfere with my ability to work the rest of the shift? (Honestly, these were questions I was asked!) I was literally sitting on both hands just to make it through the interview! I didn't want, 'strangled last interviewer in previous job search' as part of my resume. Surprise, surprise, in spite of this interview I actually did get hired.

A few years later, I ran into that same person while working in the plant. I needed to cut some strapping so I asked if he had a pair of scissors. The first thing out of his mouth, as he handed them to me was, "Why? Did you break a nail?" Silly boy! Here I am with a pair of scissors, a really good memory... and his neck is really, really close to me!

These questions are still asked in interviews with women, especially if the position is not the typical 'female' job. Men don't get asked who is looking after their children. It is assumed that has been taken care of. They do not normally get subjected to 'gender discriminatory' questions. This stereotyping must cease. It can be eliminated simply by women knowing what can and can't be asked in an interview, or what should or shouldn't carry on in the workplace.

I called in sick to work one day because my children had brought home a head full of 'unfriendly critters'. I phoned the boss and told him I wouldn't be able to come in to work because I had to clean everything up. He asked a very profound question. "Why can't your husband do that?" I didn't have an answer. The assumption was that it was the mothers' responsibility. But the reality was that there was no reason my husband couldn't have stayed home from his work and done what was needed. Typical stereotype alive and well and working in *my* home – with my permission!

The 1990's brought to light the fact that there was a huge lack of females, especially in leadership roles throughout the Working World. Companies terrified of being sued for not having 'enough' women in their employ, hired them simply to maintain the acceptable unwritten 'quota'.

Men despised women being hired or promoted over them, believing they were hired or promoted simply based on the fact that they were a woman and not because they were the best for the job. Diversity was the hot topic of the decade. Everyone was paranoid about discriminating based on gender, or religious or ethnic heritage.

Now women had another issue to contend with. Not only did we have to prove we were able to do the job and deserved equal pay for doing it, but now we had to prove we DESERVED the job or promotion based on our skills, not just because we were a woman!

As the 90's came to a close and the new millennium began, things seemed to settle down. Everyone assumed that women were now treated equally and paid equally, that diversity was no longer an issue. Sadly it wasn't - it had just been buried. New, more interesting and newsworthy issues took diversity and wage inequality's place in the headlines and the spotlight. It didn't go away - it just wasn't talked about any more. Women were making a place for themselves in the Working World; they had careers, they were earning promotions, some were reaching the top of the Corporate Ladder. It was all good.

Meanwhile, the women actually out there trying to climb up the Corporate Ladder were leaving their nail marks in every rung. Some jumped off the ladder. Some started their own business. Some just gave up while others gave in. The issue of inequality never went away. It was still alive and well, and being promoted by even the most enlightened of companies.

It is not because women don't know what they are doing. Women are not any less intelligent, less business savvy, or less capable of leading teams and Corporations or running Empires just because they are female.

We are just different. We perform tasks and solve problems differently. We think and process things differently. We still get it done and done very well but we just don't like doing it the way the men do it. Unfortunately these differences look to our male counterparts who happen to be in control, as being inefficient and non productive.

Gender differences can cause women to look less capable than men – to the men (and sadly, to some women). Unfortunately for now, men control the majority of high level positions. Men control the majority of decision making. Men use their criteria for judging who is capable and worthy – and they choose those who think and act like they do – other men.

And that is a good thing for us if we understand how they think!

If we understood some of the basics about gender differences, we could use these differences to *our advantage* when we ask for something. We could increase our chances of getting what we want. And STOP, I am not talking about wiggling certain anatomy parts, or wearing clothing that shows off your 'assets'. I am talking about professional, non-degrading, non-sexist actions that will promote a more accepting situation by the person we are negotiating with … without them even knowing it! Subtle and VERY effective!

For example:

a) Standing in front of a man to talk

If you want to talk with a man and put him at ease, never stand directly in front of him. He does not like this. To a man, this is confrontational. It means they need to be defensive. Standing side by side, shoulder to shoulder however, puts the man at ease. This is non-confrontational. I truly believe they built bars specifically to put men who are drinking at ease … notice that all the barstools are in a row shoulder to shoulder? Who would want a bunch of confrontational men in one room and under the influence of alcohol? Psychologically, sitting side by side is less aggressive for men.

When you are asking for something or want to put a man at ease before you ask, try and stand beside him, not in front of him. This will subconsciously put him in a more receptive state of mind.

The opposite applies when talking with a woman. Talk directly to her, face to face. Standing side by side makes her suspicious, as if you aren't telling her everything or are holding back information. Women like to look at the other person. We can read a lot by watching facial expressions and we like to see reactions to what we're saying. Women tend to pick up on non-verbal cues much easier and more often than men. They can judge what and how the other person is reacting to what is said and then adjust the conversation. We can't do that if we aren't facing the person.

b) Men are also very spatial (no, not spacey ... well ... never mind). They like to take up as much physical space as possible. Ever notice how men have their feet sprawled out in front of them, their arms stretched out across chairs? This is a subtle marking of their territory, the 'do not enter my space' signal. Women however, usually sit with their arms at their side or in their lap and their feet tucked under them, taking up very little space – meaning you are allowed to enter into their space much further than a man.

Don't enter a man's space unless you absolutely have to if you want to make him more compliant. If you want to be the dominant one - take up lots of room. In other words, if you are looking for a fight, get in their space. If you're not, keep out of it.

Even though a woman's space boundary allows you to be physically much closer to them, they do have limits so watch their reaction when you start to get too close – they will back up or cross their arms. This is a clear indication that you are too close.

Check it out the next time you're in the mall or a restaurant, see how often it happens. If the men get a choice, they will sit beside their companion or stand beside each other, shoulder to shoulder. Women, if given the choice will sit across from each other or their companion.

Bars now have stools that swivel. It is my personal belief they were brought in to keep women sitting up at the bar longer. They can talk directly to the person beside them just by swiveling! Smart move (even if this isn't the reason).

c) Men do not like long stories. (Retention issues? oops, sorry)

They like just the facts; short and to the point. Women like to paint a picture, get the emotions involved to emphasize a point. If you want to negotiate with a man, keep to the facts and leave out the fluff; "I want a 20% raise. I am worth it because I increased profits by 20% over the past 6 months, brought in over a million dollars in new accounts in the last two years." Stop. Pause. Breathe. Let them have a few moments to digest what you have just said. Men think in specific 'problem/solution' waves. The other stuff is just noise and gets in the way.

Here's a shopping scenario to show this more clearly that I learned from Dr. Pat Heim:

If a man wants to buy a pair of black pants, he goes to the store, finds a pair of black pants in his size, pays for them and he is done and out the door.

Most women on the other hand, want to make sure they get the 'right' black pants. We will shop from store to store, comparing the various shades of black, the feel of the material, the quality and the value. Then we make our decision. Men don't understand this – all they understand is 'black pants'. Smart malls now have sitting areas with TV (usually on the sports channel) so that the men can relax while the women search to find the 'right' pair of black pants.

When you negotiate with a man, keep it simple. You want to be clear and concise. This way the real point you are trying to make doesn't get mixed up with stuff that doesn't matter.

d) "Hi honey, how was your day?"

Okay this one is truly loaded! Men do not want to discuss their day but it's not because they don't want to talk to you. There is a more subconscious reason for this. Men only talk about problems to someone else when they have exercised all other avenues to find a solution by themselves. When a man divulges a problem he is having, he expects the other party to suggest a way to fix it.

When women discuss their problems, they don't want someone to fix it, they are perfectly capable of doing so on their own. They just want someone to listen, to empathize with them and understand where they are coming from. They want to hear the problem out loud so that a solution may come to them. So can you see the potential problem here?

Wife: "This guy at work is so lazy. I have to pull my own weight, plus his and my work is suffering."

Husband: (thinks) 'Must fix this for wife." The husband will then try to fix it, by telling her what to do.

End of communication ... and the husband is now left scratching his head because he doesn't know what made her so mad! Or ... the husband gets mad because he told her what to do... and she didn't take his advice! The other side of the coin is this: If the man states a problem and the woman doesn't respond with a solution... well, you can see where this one is headed. Translation: she obviously doesn't know what to do about it so end the conversation and I'll go ask Bob.

There, now you know; it's not the man's fault!

- When you ask 'how was your day', and you get a grunt of 'fine,' it's not because they don't want to talk to you. They are just not willing to have someone else 'fix' whatever it is yet. Or there is nothing to 'fix' therefore, no conversation needs to be discussed.

- If they ask *you* how your day was ... be gentle; stick to facts, and try not to lead them to thinking they need to fix something for you.

- In the workplace, when you ask 'how is Project B coming along', a lack of a lengthy answer from a man is not a personal affront, it's just the 'no need for a solution'.

- If they bring a problem to you, know that they are expecting your input on how to solve it.

Finally, a little nugget; when you offer a solution, phrasing it as a question can help. "What do you think, would it work if you did this?" It will make your input less condescending or threatening. When they answer the question, it will see to them like they thought of it themselves. This way they can save face and still take credit for the solution (hint: they will anyway – that's coming up).

e) Nodding your head.

This is a canon just waiting to be fired!

Men before a meeting or brain storming session will go around to all those attending the session and explain his idea of how to fix the issue that's going to be discussed. He will collect their responses to his idea, mentally counting the number of 'yes's and those 'on his side'.

Imagine this:

Bill approaches Sally and tells her he has a great idea for the brainstorming session. Sally nods her head, listening to Bill. In the session, Bill brings up his solution to the issue. Sally says they need to hear from everyone else first before making any decisions. What? Bill is thinking, but she agreed with me earlier! I told her my idea, and she nodded her head! Now she's changing her mind! What's going on with her?

Sally actually never **agreed** with Bill. When women nod their head, they are not necessarily agreeing with you, they are just letting you know that yes, they are listening to you and hear what you are saying.

When men nod their head it is like a hand shake. Yes, I agree with you. So you can see the problem when men and women are discussing issues, and the woman is nodding her head! Be careful when you do this, make it clear that yes you hear what they are saying, but not necessarily agreeing with them. Try NOT to nod your head – unless of course, you are speaking with a woman. Then by all means, nod away, otherwise she will think you are not listening!

f) It has been proven that men's brains can actually 'flat line'. They can go into a total 'dead' zone where literally the brain is doing absolutely nothing. Women's brains however never shut down, which is most likely why we are the experts at multi-tasking. Our brain functions by having multiple 'files' opened at the same time. We can work on one file, pull something from another while a third file is waiting for more data. All our files are interconnected. Picture a file cabinet with thousands of drawers, and 25% of them are open. This is a women's brain. Men have their files in separate cabinets, thousands of individual cabinets with one or two files in each. They are not connected. If they close that cabinet and nothing else is opened, you get - the dead zone.

Women can have several things on the go at the same time, several drawers opened simultaneously. They never have all the drawers closed and some drawers are always open.

Outwardly to a man, this looks like totally inefficient, absolute chaos, disorganized and unproductive. 'Lynda, you have too much on your plate' was a constant complaint by a Manager that I worked for, yet for me it was when I would do my best work. It meant I had to be ultra organized and efficient with my time. It meant that I could be flexible and was adaptable to sudden changes, and could accommodate multiple priorities. These are GREAT leadership qualities. These are qualities that women inherently have in abundance. These are qualities that are now being actively sought after by Corporations.

Men don't understand how anything can be accomplished unless you focus on one thing at a time. Men deal with that one thing until it's finished and only then do they move on to the next project or issue. Ever wondered why men can fight and argue like sailors, and then go have a beer together? They had a problem, they solved the problem, somebody won, somebody lost. It's all done and taken care of – the file drawer is closed. Then they **let it go**! Otherwise they wouldn't be able to focus on something else. It is forgotten and they move on. Period.

We women NEVER let it go, the file is NEVER closed. It is merely put away in the 'to be brought up again at another time in the future' folder in our brain. Remember, the file drawer is never closed and the files are interconnected. This means that this file could come back up at *any* time.

The flat zone in men simply means they really don't hear you. Now when you ask if they are listening to you and they don't answer … well, put it down to them being in their 'dead' zone.

g) Women should not have to act like a man to get paid like a man.

We do not have to act, look, or behave like a man, or 'grow a set' to get where we want to go. We need to educate ourselves, our colleagues, our employers, and society that we can achieve the same successful results albeit through different styles.

Long overdue for retirement is the hierarchy of one leader; the Big Boss–little-servant leadership; do as I say with no questions asked, I am King and everything flows downhill from here.

Until now, women have had to follow the only rules in the game – the men's rules. Women need to create a set of their own rules, rules that will be comfortable to execute and comfortable for others to accept. We need to stop playing by the men's rules and start doing what is right for us and for the new generation of the Working World. This is true whether you are an employee or run your own business or Corporation.

The first Rule is to start speaking up and asking for what we want! We can use the differences between men and women to our advantage – without any guilt, without demeaning ourselves or not being true to who we are. We still want everyone to feel like they have gained something in the negotiation and we want to ask for what we want with the least amount of confrontation. Now we know how to use gender differences to 'help' that along.

Stereotype notwithstanding, here is something to remind us of how truly powerful we are:

'The hand that rocks the cradle is the hand that rules the world' -WW Ross. (1819-1881) We've always known that, now let's get out there and show the world!

4. THE GOOD GIRL SYNDROME

AKA

THE NEED TO PLEASE

"If we make sure everyone is happy, then we are happy!" This has been the lullaby sung by women for centuries. This was to be our purpose in life and was drilled into us from birth – duty and loyalty unto others before ourselves. This is what a 'good' girl does, and this is what you are here to do. A young girl did not come out of a conversation unscathed if she said she was going to do something for herself, be what *she* wanted to be, especially if it did not fit in to the normal pattern of what a woman should do. She was ostracized, criticized and avoided.

Did you know that Switzerland was the last Western Republic to give women the right to vote in a federal election – in 1973? I had already graduated high school and was working full time – and some women were just getting the right to vote! So it appears that we haven't come such a long way, baby.

Most women still generally follow instructions, keep a low profile and try to say "yes" to anything and everything that is asked of us – to the expense of what we want for ourselves. Even if it means we have no room, no time or no desire to do so, we will try to accommodate a request. We do all the nasty stuff that no-one else wants to take on. We let people keep piling it on until we are buried.

Then it is our fault if it doesn't get done, or it's not done right. Overwhelmed and afraid to ask for help, lest we look less than capable, we quit or take another position, or work longer and harder just to keep up which again, makes us look incompetent.

While raising 3 school aged children, nurturing a baby, taking care of a husband and our home plus working full time 12 hour shifts, I became overwhelmed (do ya think??)

I was tired of asking for help, and not getting it. 12 loads of laundry – please take one load out of the washer and put it in the dryer – how hard can this be? Apparently too hard – 3 days later when I have a 'day off', go to do more laundry and there is the load, still in the washer – and NOT smelling too pretty. Ugh!

On overload, I went on strike! I refused to wash the pile of dishes in the sink, (never understood this because we had a dishwasher), vacuum, dust, or do laundry. I quit! There were 4 other very capable persons in the house to help out. They could do it for a change.

The kids went to school with dirty socks and mud cover pants. Hubby had to iron his own shirts (which was okay, because I never did them right anyway). The dust piled up on the TV screen. And I waited. And waited.

Nothing. Well, that's not entirely true; a note from school asking me if there were problems at home because the children's clothes weren't clean and did I want to be referred to someone who could help me with parenting skills and proper hygiene (translation – my fault). The neighbours brought their own coffee mugs, because I didn't have any clean ones. (What a lazy, sloppy housekeeper.) Hubby pitched right in – by staying late at work until the kids were in bed so he didn't have to hear the whining.

It didn't work, in fact it totally backfired! It was a total reflection on MY lack of responsibility, MY housekeeping skills or lack thereof, and MY attitude. The whispers were, "She took on this project called marriage and family and it's up to her to look after it. She should quit whining and get back to it!" Some friends and neighbours were sympathetic and actually found it amusing. Not! (Funny that they are the ones who are still my friends…) So, not only did I not make the point I was trying to make, I just created even more work for myself and had to walk the Housekeeping Hall of Shame.

The more we do, the more we are asked to do and the more we say 'yes', until there is no 'us' left to give… then we take on a little more.

Social scientists Myra and David Sadker found that girl students receive less praise for the intellectual quality of their ideas, and are taught to value neatness over innovation. They are rewarded for being nice.

Margaret Thatcher was called the Iron Lady. Hillary Clinton was continuously vilified for being so 'pushy'. Names such as hard-nosed, tenacious, manly, bull dog all found their way into newsprint when describing her. It was front page news because a reporter photographed her as she was shedding a tear - this was newsworthy because?? It will be reported more on what women are wearing than what they are saying. Women in the media must be impeccably dressed, coiffed and made up at all times. A male news reporter can report in track pants or shorts and it's all good.

Bad girls are what the boys like to play with – good girls are the ones they take home to Mama.

Now take this centuries-old attitude into the Board Room. Good girls sit there and take notes while the 'big' boys conduct business. If we try to add our ideas into the discussions we can either be ignored or seem to have insulted them somehow.

I was in a workshop once with my coworkers. During one exercise we were divided into groups. Each group formed a circle with one person holding a ball. The object of the exercise was that everyone in the group had to touch a ball; the first group to do so would win. I asked the facilitator if we could all touch the ball at the same time. (Looking for validation of my idea which women do SO often.) He just smiled but said nothing. I mentioned it to the group. No response. One male member heard me, and said to the group, 'Hey! Everybody, touch the ball at the same time!

We won, he was patted on the back and cheered by all the group – except me. I stood there with my mouth open in total disbelief and said nothing. The facilitator then asked the group who had heard my suggestion. No-one had heard me. (I know ONE person did).

When the Facilitator told them that I was the first one to suggest that everyone touch the ball at the same time but nobody had listened to me, they didn't believe him. Do you know what the point of the exercise was? Listening to everyone's point of view and ideas because everyone has something valuable to share. I learned a big lesson that day; speak up.

In 'The Curse of the Good Girl' written by Rachel Simmons, she argues that women pressure themselves to fit the mold of modest, selfless, rule-following good girl for fear of being labelled a 'bitch'. If we stand out, speak up and are strong, we are punished for it. It's a double standard. Those *very* attributes that get most men a pat on the back and a promotion only get women labels. A woman who stays late, comes in earlier must not have a clue what she's doing or has problems at home. A man doing the same thing? Wow! What a go-getter, he'll go far in this company!

Women who make their own rules, take big chances, toot their own horns and don't worry if everyone likes them, do get ahead according to Kate White, author of Why Good Girls Don't Get Ahead But Gutsy Girls Do. But how comfortable were they getting there? According to most highly successful women, they had to fight their way to get where they are, and they didn't like it one bit. Many of these women also realized that all the way up the ladder, they were still making less than their male colleagues, and yet they didn't say anything!

Here is an interesting statistic I pulled from a report by Business in Vancouver. Of the top 100 highest paid executives in BC (2010) in total compensation:

# 7	John Currie	CFO of Lululemon Athletica	$9,192,002
#10	Christine Day	CEO of Lululemon Athletica	$7,529,044
#54	Sheree Waterson	Exec. VP Lululemon Athletica	$2,776,189
#90	Elaine Wong	Exec VP Westport Innovations	$1,805,641

First, there are only 3 women in the top 100. Second, just my personal observation and opinion - that in the Company Lululemon, the male still makes the most money... almost $2,000,000 more as a CFO than the CEO! There could be many reasons unknown to me why this is true. But looking at stats like this, it's not comforting. Women do make it to the top, but not very fast, or in great numbers and most likely make less than a colleague in an equal position.

So, what to do, what to do? Do we turn from being the good girl, into the bitch and fight our way up the ladder? Do we resign ourselves to being the good girl and accept what is given? Or can we have it all? I think we can have it all, or pretty darn close if we follow some guidelines:

1. Please remove the doormat from your forehead. This area will no longer be open for others to walk over.
2. Practice saying "No." Start with the dog, the kids, the hubby, then the school committees, neighbours, girlfriends. Then move on up to the bigger stuff – volunteer group, workmates, clients, colleagues and then the boss.
3. Start letting people know what is already on your plate. "No, I can't take on another project until my other 20 are completed, thanks for asking."
4. Another way to say no is, "Certainly I can take on that project. Which of the other 20 would you like me to pass on to someone else so I can take care of that for you?"
5. How about, "Right now I have 3 projects that you want completed 'now'. Which 'now' project would you like me to complete first? This one I have found to be extremely effective.

Are you thinking, "If I say I can't do something they will think I can't do my job"? If they are aware of what you are doing, working on and working toward, this won't be an issue and you can always give them a gentle reminder. Make sure they know what you are doing – while you are doing it! Do not start with a long list of reasons why you can't do something, that is being defensive. You have nothing to defend. Your plate is full, you cannot take on any more without removing or delegating something.

But what if it is a career making opportunity? Before you say no, or you can't - can you delegate other tasks in order to take on that great opportunity? You could say something like this: "I'd love the opportunity to do that. In fact, I can turn this and that over to so-and-so, which will leave room for me to do this exciting project, will that work for you?"

This one may be a really hard one (it certainly was for me). Let go. Delegate. Great leaders do NOT do all the work themselves. They find the right people to do the job. Then they let them do it! If you don't have faith in your staff to do what they are there to do, why are they there? You will be amazed at how much time you can free up to do the things that matter to you, when you let go of the things that don't, especially those things that you hate to do! Why not find someone who loves to do the things you hate to do?

What is your mantra? Do the math, right? If you are spending time doing $10/hr. stuff, you are not spending it on the $200/hr. stuff. Hire/delegate someone for the $10/hr stuff – and then let them do it.

There may be a little 'flack' and grumbling at first, as you begin saying no but soon others will learn to come to you when they *need* to and not just to pass the buck because they know you won't say no. You aren't just changing your way of doing things, but others' expectations of you, so try to be gentle with them until they get used to the new-and-improved you.

NOTE: Be mindful whether the person that you are delegating to does not already have too much on *their* plate.

I worked with a line leader once that said, "I don't have to like you to work with you". I thought that was just about the most hurtful thing to say to someone. Everyone was supposed to like me; that was what I spent all my time trying to create – the relationship! Now I realize he was right. I was there to do a job, and be the best I could be doing it.

It would be great if everyone liked each other and worked together to get things done in harmony but for every 100 people, there are 100 personalities, 100 different beliefs and 100 different perceptions. It's not going to be harmonious all the time.

I try to hire people that are the 'right' fit for my Company, my personality and my values which lessens the major differences and creates a much more productive working environment.

The bottom line is – I can work with any-one as long as I respect them – but they don't have to be my new best friend. I don't have to worry about hurting their feelings by not taking on more than I can handle effectively.

If you are in business for yourself take a look at your clients and see how many of them are creating extra 'this isn't making any money' work for you. Are they causing you to have too much on your plate?

Remember the 80/20 Rule. 80% of your sales/profits come from 20% of your clients. Decide which clients you want to work with and start weeding out the rest. I read where a woman really did not want to take on a certain 'high maintenance' client so she tripled her fees just so they wouldn`t hire her – but they did! That caused her to take a look at her fees overall. She then used this as the catalyst to start raising her fees by immediately doubling them for all new clients – successfully and letting her current clients know she would be raising their fee, with little fallout. You can fire a client. You can say no.

Learning to say no does not make you a bad person. Being able to delegate may even help you to skip a couple rungs on the ladder. It shows others that you respect yourself, that you recognize that your time is just as important as everyone else's, that what you do matters just as much as what they do. And if you have to start firing clients, do so. You can still be a good girl … only now a brilliant and savvy 'good' girl!

So why do I hear your little voice saying, "Ya, but…"

5. SELF DISCRIMINATION –

OUR OWN LOW EXPECTATIONS

We expect less right from the beginning. If you ask most women what they think they will make at the peak of their career, their answers are generally 30% lower than what men will answer. With a salary range we work our way up – to the middle.

I submitted a resume for an Insurance Company for a "Customer Service" position (which turned out to be a Sales position). As soon as I walked into their office building, I was over whelmed. 'Posh' is putting it mildly! This was one high class, professional building, and something I had NEVER been exposed to.

I immediately told myself this was WAY out of my league. I instantly decided that I wasn't good enough to work there. This office oozed success and I certainly wasn't in the same category. All the staff passing in the hall were draped in clothing that most likely cost more than my annual salary! My skill level confidence meter suddenly plummeted. I just wanted to get out of there as fast as I could. I did not belong there.

Filling out the application made it crystal clear that I was in the wrong place. "Did I expect to be a manager within 2 years?" I actually said 'no' to this. My (low self esteem) thinking was, they weren't going to spend money to train me in the position I had applied for and then have me move on (silly me).

Needless to say, the interview was a disaster. I hadn't researched the Company or the position I was applying for. It was a field outside anything I had ever done before and I hadn't bothered to research this either. After months of looking for work and not finding anything, I was just desperate for a job, and willing to do anything (legal). I literally talked myself out of the job, without any help from the interviewer. I couldn't wait for the interview to end and I'm sure he felt the same way.

Over the next few days, I thought about all the benefits that the Company was offering and the opportunities for advancement, potential income and freedom that working for this Company would have given me. I sat down and step by step went through their skill requirements and realized that I DID have the skills for the position and more. In fact I would have been a definite asset to the Company! I got mad at myself for letting the opportunity slip away.

About 2 months later I saw the ad again. I applied again explaining who I was and that I had previously been interviewed for the position. I thought what the heck, all they can do is say no or not even respond. I also added that since the last interview, I had researched the Company and assessed my skills and believed that I would definitely be the right fit for their Company. They were the kind of Company I could build a career with and one that I wanted to work for.

Two weeks went by. Although I didn't hear from them it felt good that I had taken charge and done something. And then the Company called. I got another chance. In fact, the interviewer was so impressed that I had asked for a second chance; he said he'd never had this happen before, and the interview was mine to conduct because he didn't know how! This time I was not overwhelmed. I was confident both in the job and myself and it showed. I knew what I was worth to the Company. I knew I could do the job. And that gave me the boost to go after what I wanted.

I got the job.

Although other 'things' happened and I ended up not taking the position, it was amazing how much power it gave me, how much it increased my self-esteem and self confidence to shed the low expectation I had of myself and go after something I wanted.

A few years later I walked into another building with marble floors, high class décor, and I smiled as I recalled the Insurance Company job. This time I didn't let it intimidate me and I knew I belonged there, because in fact I did – I worked there!

We are always promoting someone else and putting ourselves down in the process. We start out on the low end of a scale with the hopes of hitting the middle. We expect to get less – and we do. This just validates the thought that we deserve less.

If there is a salary range, where do you put yourself on that scale? I would put myself on the low end, even though the high end was what attracted me to the position in the first place. This was my thought process: they'll probably offer me the low end, but if I'm lucky I'll get the mid range. I would never think to ask for the highest range or perhaps ABOVE the highest.

Sometimes I would find an ad with a Company that had a great reputation to work for and the job was very attractive, but I wouldn't apply because they advertised a salary that was lower than what I wanted. All those missed opportunities just because I wouldn't think to negotiate.

What if I had stated my salary expectation even though higher, with one of those Companies? If I don't ask, I'm no worse off than before ... or am I? If I had shown them why I was the best candidate and worth the extra few dollars they may have hired me - but I'll never know - because I didn't ask.

We have to stop shooting ourselves in our bank account. We deserve at the very *least* equal what the market is willing to pay. We deserve more if we can offer the Company more.

Repeat: "I deserve this. I am asking for what I deserve. I am asking for what I am worth!

As an entrepreneur or business owner, wages aren't the issue for you. You have to research your client's market. You have to know what your client type is currently paying others and what they are willing to pay for services/products like yours. You have to know what the competition offers and what they are getting for the same services.

Do you or have you ever:

- Offered the client a lower rate at the very beginning?

- Immediately accept what the client says they want to pay? Why?

- Offered a discount if they look like they are going to walk away?

- How often do you lower your rates, even though you know your product or service is worth what you originally asked for?

- Do you mentally discount before the 'price process' even starts?

- Do you give them extra bonuses?

- Do you know what discounts other business owners are getting from suppliers?

- Do you ask for those same discounts?

You have choices to make. You can sell your services/products at market or below market value, or you can show why your service or product is worth more ... why YOU are worth more and why they should pay for the value you bring because it is the best, it exceeds all others in the market.

"You get what you pay for". If your clients don't care about the product as much as the price, do you want them for a client? You are in business to solve your client's problems, to show them they have a problem, and that you can fix it. The better you can do that, the more the solution is worth. Stop thinking lowest to middle and start thinking highest and above!

Do the math.

If you are going to compete strictly on a dollar for dollar basis with the rest of the market, then you have to be the lowest, or equal to the lowest or you have to offer discounts or bonuses. You will then attract those clients that are only looking for the cheapest price and not necessarily the best service or product. Who do you want to attract? If you are an expert in your field with a highly sought after, hard-to-find product or service, or something that is unique, and you are the only one offering it, *you* set the value and establish what your product/service is worth because there is nothing out there to compare it to. Pricing is yours to create! You set the bar – not just for your business but the market. You are the expert. You are the *leading* expert. Your skill, service, or product is the one the client needs and will have to meet the value you place on that product or service.

Take away their choices. Make yours the *only* logical solution to their problem – and then get paid for it.

This is all any of us are doing, whether as an employee, employer, or business owner. We are the solution, or we have the solution to their problem. The only thing we need to figure out is how much are they willing to pay us to solve their problem?

Often, we lower our own expectations of ourselves, what we can do, what we are worth, or how valuable we could be - until we end up where we think *they* think we belong, or where we have been told we belong. Here's what many women tend to do:

John, the Manager comes to you and says that there is a new position coming up that he thinks you would be really good at. It's a promotion with a lot more responsibility, perks, benefits and pay. It is ground breaking stuff, the kind of project that dream careers are built on. It's something that you have never even thought of doing before. You would have to learn some new skills very quickly and step into a whole new world.

The first thing you do is this: Who me? You think I could do something like that? I don't know. But hey, you know who would be really great at that? Bob. Bob could do that job really well. You should ask him!

Putting others before us is inherent in our DNA. We have to blow those little molecules and atoms up! We downplay what we do and what we can do, so that we 'fit in' to the stereotype. We self-discriminate, take ourselves out of the running in order to promote someone else.

STOP DOING THAT!

From today… never, never, never put yourself or your abilities down. When someone notices or compliments your work, your skills anything, from now on you say, "Thank you", and then you shut up! (I hope that was not too blunt).

There is more than one reason for this. The first is obvious. Do not take the recognition away from yourself. It is hard for a lot of women to accept praise, sometimes it's because they don't feel they deserve it. Sometimes it's because they now feel 'obligated' to return it, so they don't owe the other person anything.

Another very important reason is that you validate the other person's assessment of you or whatever they were praising or complimenting. When you disagreed with what they said, or immediately feel the need to reciprocate, you take their compliment and throw it away into the garbage.

(Them): "Love your dress".

(You): "What, this old thing? I got it at a yard sale for like $2".

In reality, you are telling them their compliment doesn't mean anything to you, even though that wasn't your intent. Stop doing that.

From now on we will graciously accept what is given, we will become excellent receivers when it comes to acknowledgement and compliments. We may not get them a lot in the workplace, so enjoy them when one comes our way!

A funny thing tends to happen when we do. We get more. The more open to receiving you are, the more you will receive. Keep giving to others but make sure you let them give too!

Another little bonus? You can use their compliments or recognition to let others know that 'so-and-so' thinks your work is outstanding! You are not bragging about your work – someone else is! You can do it in a very casual way by saying something like, "I just got the nicest compliment from …." which takes any boasting or self-serving feeling away.

Yes, you have to toot your own horn. Yes, you have to let others know your accomplishments. Women are experts at doing this for others. First, you have to acknowledge that you HAVE skills and talents and that you deserve to be recognized for them. Raise your bar!

If you must, when you first start, pretend that you are someone else and you are promoting their qualities. Think of yourself in the 3rd person. If you knew someone that had all your talent, what would you say about them? What would you tell them that would help them get what they want? How would you help them? Then go do it!

We will now honor EVERY thing we do, have and are. Repeat after me… "I am great at what I do. I deserve this because I am the best. I know my stuff". Do for yourself what you would gladly and selflessly do for others.

Please sound the horns! The 'ya buts' have left the building..........

Lynda Hykin

6. ACHIEVEMENTS –

OUR BIGGEST KEPT SECRET

I used to take public transit to work. In fact, I spent 780 hours a year, which is 32.5 days of my life sitting on either a train or a bus travelling back and forth to work. I believe this makes me qualified to share my observations. This is how I travelled on a typical day, and noticed that so did most women:

I have the purse and/or backpack (I lived in Vancouver, BC and backpacks are considered a fashionable necessity), which contains the lunch bag, makeup bag, and all the paraphernalia required for the day. Then I have the 'carry-on' bag, which holds the free newspapers (there are several), the shoes, the book I may get a chance to read should I snag a seat, and the empty bag because I am going grocery shopping after work and I'm environmentally conscious. The men taking transit carry - the wallet. Period. Granted, some men do have a lap top case or backpack, but mostly just the wallet.

This 'difference' in what we drag around with us seems to carry (I do like puns) over into the workplace. Let me give you a scenario that shows this:

The Suitcase of Success

Sally has finally had enough! She has just been passed over for a promotion – again. Sally has worked her butt off for this Company for the past 10 years and yet she is still struggling to advance her career. She hasn't been given the opportunities to work on big career building projects, earn bonuses or promotions, and she knows for a fact she is making less than her male colleagues.

Just at that moment Sally spies her boss coming down the hall and tells him she wants a word with him. He checks his watch and says he has a few minutes before his next appointment.

Sally goes in to this impromptu meeting (clue) dragging this huge mental suitcase with her that contains **every**thing she has ever done for the Company in the last 10 years!

She starts telling him every single thing she has achieved or accomplished. She verbally hauls out her awards, certificates and diplomas. She lists all the improvements she has made, the reduction of waste, the increase in production or sales.

Have you ever seen a Charlie Brown show? Whenever the grown-ups are talking it's all distorted, like "whah-whah-whah-whah-whah." Well that is exactly what Sally's boss is hearing right now. He has stopped listening. His mind is now only focused on how to get out of there! And he's terrified this tirade will lead to the shedding of tears! He is praying for the phone to ring, the secretary to rush in with a crisis, the fire alarm to go off, *any* distraction!

And … he … doesn't … even … know … what … she … wants!

Sally has just sabotaged herself – twice.
The first was telling him what she has done over the past 10 years – in 10 seconds! The second and more damaging was that she had been hoarding all of her successes to herself, hiding all her achievements in the 'success' suitcase only to have the suitcase explode.

Most women keep their accomplishments to themselves. They don't tell others. We do this because it would seem tasteless, self-serving and it sounds like boasting or bragging. Good girls don't do that. We quietly go about creating our success. We just don't like to talk about it. It's how we were raised. Even if your mom told you that you could be anything or do anything, it was always understood that we had to do it nicely - and quietly.

And so we stash away what we *really* do. We put it somewhere in our minds under "Save for later". It all gets filed away along with everything we have ever accomplished in our life in the filing cabinet.

I will bet if you wrote down everything you do in a week and then asked your boss to write down what you do, his list would be a whole lot shorter than yours. Actually, try it, just for fun! I'd love to know the outcome!

How is the boss supposed to know what you do or what you've done? He is busy creating his own career and most likely not paying too much attention to yours. We have to tell them.

Men, the darlings, have no problem with this. They tell you what they've done, what they're doing, and even what they are *going* to do, *with the expectation of recognition and reward.* They don't store anything up. This is why they travel so 'lightly'.

Ladies, we need to lighten our load. We need to start emptying our 'success' suitcase, one accomplishment at a time, as it happens. Less baggage being dragged around means more energy for other things. We deserve the recognition and reward for what we have achieved and we deserve to be compensated for it. But we won't get it if no-one knows about it.

We are usually so busy 'doing' that we don't get a chance to promote our stuff. We figure everyone should already know what we're doing, and they will bring the reward to us. We wait for the recognition that is sure to come for a job well done. Then we wonder why we didn't get it. And all those passed-over-for things just keep getting filed away – until BOOM! The file drawer topples over! If we let it out a little at a time, this won't happen, and there won't be any 'clean up on aisle seven' to worry about.

We do have reasons for keeping it to ourselves. One of those is opportunity. In the Working World women don't have the same opportunities to let others know what they're doing like men do. Men go out after work and have a beer. Women go home and do laundry. Men network, hang out on the golf course and get all the juicy 'happening' information. Women go home, cook, clean and make lunches.

Women don'' *make* time for networking and socializing outside the office. Unfortunately, this is where stuff gets done, where men get to let others know about their accomplishments (and how much they got), to find out who is doing what, where the openings, the opportunities, the big changes coming down the pipe are. Women get the notice when it's posted. By the time you decide you might like to take that new position, it's all but been decided.

Make the time. Period. A couple hours once a week, is just a couple of hours in time, but priceless in career boosting. I book nothing, and do nothing on Tuesday nights. That is my networking night. Even if a scheduled meet-up is cancelled, I find somewhere to network. It is not open for compromise or rescheduling. Make that commitment to yourself. You owe it to yourself. A night out with the girls at the office, a function, a play day with staff – go! You either have reasons or results. Bolster your determination with your 'why'. My daughter actually thought it was weird but awesome, that Mom did something at night outside of being a Mom.

Women don't need to pompously brag but we need to get our stuff out there, let people - the right people, know what we have done, what we are working on and what we want the opportunity to do. Oh, while I`m at it, when you DO get recognized please don`t do this:

(Sally) 'Thank you, but it wasn't me, it was a group effort, everyone contributed to making this happen." Be more like the guys on this one:

(Bill) "Thanks! Not only was this an incredible success, I have another lead that I'm working on that will be an even bigger deal than this last one."

Acknowledge deserved recognition with a thank you. It is okay to identify and recognize the others on the team that helped **you** to accomplish the goal or achievement, without taking away from your part. I know, I know, this is really a hard one. But try.

New rules:

> Share what you have done, what you are doing, and what you intend to do.
>
> Share what is bothering you directly to the person that can actually *do* something with the information you are sharing.
>
> Share where you want to go with your business or your career ... with those that can help you get there. The family dog is totally devoted to you and hangs on every word you say ... but he can't get you the promotion or the pay raise or that client that will take your business to a new level.
>
> Share with those that can actually help. Save the commiserating for the girlfriends over Mohitos.

Understand that we have to tell those in control what we want.

Which could be ...

Lynda Hykin

7. WORK-LIFE BALANCE

IT'S NOT EITHER/OR –

IT'S A BARGAINING TOOL

Reports from Statistics Canada show that while men are doing more household chores and women are doing more paid work, men still spend only 1.4 hours per day on housework compared to the 2.4 hours done by women. Women are also in the majority when it comes to nurturing and taking care of the children.

I know so well the guilt attached to a Mom choosing between work and spending those precious, never-to-get-back-again years with their little one. Dragging a baby out at 5am in the middle of winter to cart off to the babysitter, then not picking them up until almost their bedtime. Missing out on the first time they fell off the couch; the first time they said a certain 'bad' word; leaving them screaming in someone else's arms as they reach for Mommy, who doesn't care and is still leaving them behind; then the same child screaming because big bad Mommy won't let them stay just a little longer at the sitters.

We make decisions about how to share those few precious hours after supper - between cooking, housework (okay this one I admit, was not a priority for me-ever), lunches, homework, hockey, skating, school plays, the husband and the children. There's never enough time. And it's our fault (so we think). We are a bad Mom because we have chosen to fulfill something within us, a career. Perhaps we must leave them to make sure there is food on the table. Either way, no matter how we justify it – we make the choices. We want to be the best in both worlds. If things get rough, we feel we have to make a sacrifice of one for the other.

Now that it is just me on my own, my daughter having started her own family, I have different choices and decisions that weigh heavily in the work or stay home scenario. Now my quandary is more like this:

I would really rather be sitting on the beach with a very cold beverage beside me, the warm, turquoise blue water in front of me and the hot sun behind me heating my skin with its toasty rays.

My laptop and cell would be the only equipment I require as I conduct business from my new 'office' aka the beach. Ah, can't you just picture it? Decisions, decisions.

Do I retire, just work part time, or live on my savings and pension? Should I start my own business so that I have the freedom to do what I want, when I want? (running your own business does not automatically come with those benefits by the way).

Do I work from home one or two days a week? Can I work 4 10 hour days so I can have an extra day off?

Anyone out there ever heard of something called "ME" time?? Negotiation is not just about money, promotions or career moves. It is about the lifestyle you want and about living how you want, whatever that is. This is your life and you deserve to live it as you choose.

If you want more family time, then ask for it. Use it as your why when you negotiate your contract. More and more companies are coming to realize the '9-5' and 'must work in a cubby hole' is not always the most effective work environment. With the technology that we have, we can virtually conduct business anywhere in the world – including the beach!

Determine what your personal and professional goals are:

What would your ideal job/career/life look like?

- Part time hours with full time income?
- Working from home a few days a week?
- Flexible hours so you can attend the family's important events?

Work-life Balance is achieved when you can live a fulfilled life at work, at home and in society, when the choices you make are accepted and respected. The only way this will be accomplished is if you are making the decisions, the choices. You have to make the rules. You have to let others know what you want, what you are willing and not willing to do. Do not let your boss, colleagues or co-workers make assumptions about this.

Will you travel? Don't let them assume you won't just because you have a family. I travelled extensively – to the enjoyment of my family. They loved it when I went away so they could relax, eat from the pot without benefit of dishes, most likely stay up really, really late (although this was never admitted to), and not have to clean up until I was on my way home. They got special bonding time when Mom was away which brought them closer together. It also made coming home more enjoyable and appreciated. While away, I got to relax in a tub filled with bubbles, candles on the side, a good book and a glass of red wine, soft music and absolutely NO-ONE pounding on the door, demanding they have to go NOW. Yes, I loved to travel and I made sure my boss knew it. I would accept ANY opportunity to travel for the company.

Work-life balance has major benefits for the boss and the company as well. They include:

- Increased productivity. I love this one! When I work, I can give it 110% because I don't have other things pulling me in two or twenty different directions.
- Retain skilled employees. A happy employee is an employee that stays with the Company.
- Lower rates of absenteeism. I don't need those 'sick' days to attend my child's concert.
- A more motivated, satisfied and committed worker who is more engaged in their results and the Company's profit and success because it also leads to their success.

Lynda Hykin

8. THE WORD 'NO'

Did you know, there are really 3 no`s?

> a. No, not now
> b. No, not ever
> c. Do I know someone or a Company that will give me what I want?

No is not the final answer. Its only the opening line. It's just the starting point.

Here is a typical discussion:

(Me) I have been here for several years now. I was wondering if I could perhaps get a little more money for the extra work I've been doing?

(Boss) No.

(Me) Oh, okay. Um, why not?

(Boss) It's not in the budget, and your contract doesn't come up for another six months.

(Me) Okay, well could we perhaps discuss it again when my contract is due for renewal?

(Boss) We'll see how you are doing then.

(Me) Okay, sorry to bother you.

(Me) I leave the office with my tail between my legs. I'm embarrassed that I had to ask. This makes me mad. Fine! If he isn't going to give me a raise,

I'm outta here!

I start looking – I leave.

Like shampoo I repeat as necessary.

Let's pick this apart a bit.

I went in asking a question, not making a statement. Many women tend to ask in questions, which makes them appear uncertain and insecure. We end our sentences with our voice rising…as if asking, not stating a fact.

I did not have a *short,* relevant list of the tasks I'm doing without compensation that I want to be paid for.

My contract isn't up yet. I should have known when my contract was up. Then I might have gone in like this, "What if we review my contract now and create an addendum to it, so that these inclusions can be implemented when it does come up?" If I wait until the new contract comes around – the budget may already have been set, and the 'no' will seem valid - again.
Note to self: When is the budget up?

I went in there not really expecting to get anything – and that's exactly what I got. I considered his no as the final answer. Do you know or have you ever seen ANY child stop asking after the first no? They are masters at negotiating! (And how many times have you given in just to get on with what you were doing?)

I did not go in with a specific (researched) amount. I want 'X' dollars/time off/in lieu/etc. We have to give them an opening 'bid' or starting figure. That figure should ALWAYS be much higher than what you actually want, so that you have 'wiggle' room. If you start with exactly what you want and they say no, you have begun the negotiation process with no room to negotiate TO GET what you want – and you will now walk away with less – guaranteed. Even if this higher amount seems ridiculous to you, do it anyway. He laughs or blows up – 'are you kidding me? That amount is ridiculous!' Then you get to very calmly slide in the "okay, so what amount do you think is fair?"

You have just begun the negotiating process! See how easy that was? I know, I know, but it will get easier, trust me. Picture it like badminton or volley ball game. You serve (I want). They volley (no). You return it. (What would they consider) and back and forth.

NEVER let your emotions enter into to any negotiating process. Leave them outside the door – you can pick them up on the way out. Remember 'no' is not a personal affront against you. It is just a word.

Find out what 'no' you have been given. If it's no, not now – when? Then negotiate the when. You can use this quite effectively; less now, more later, none now and a lot more later, or equal now and later.

This is so much fun! Get creative! Negotiating is about having both sides get what they want. That's all. It's not cut and dried. It's ever evolving. If you encourage them to give their input and ensure them that their opinion of the situation is valued you will go a lot further toward a successful conclusion.

Treat 'no, not ever' the same way. "What if"…. is always a great way to diffuse the 'no, not ever' scenario. Again, remember, you are solving a problem for them and need to be justly compensated for it, whether it's a client, a boss, the car dealer, anyone. You know what they need because you've done your research. You know what it's worth and can verify that your request is not out of line.

When the no is not moving anywhere. When you have expired all avenues to turn the no into a yes, maybe, or anything other than just dangling in the air, you need to know your BATNA.

What the heck is BATNA you ask?

BATNA stands for Best Alternative To a Negotiated Agreement.

This is otherwise known as Plan B.

Never go into a negotiation without a Plan B. You have to know:

- What is your bottom line?

Determine what figure will you absolutely not go below but keep it to yourself. Do NOT change this! This is part of your core values. This is part of your self-worth. This is the big part of your 'why'. Find your bottom line and stick to it. If you are wishy-washy here, you're lost - it's over - for clients, bosses, suppliers, anyone.

And please, never, ever say "I will not go below $X." out loud. I actually said this once - at the BEGINNING. Guess what I got? Yep - $X, which was my BOTTOM line and not what I really wanted. This figure is only for you, to keep close to your chest and not ever revealed.

- At what point do you walk away?

Beating a dead horse just makes for tired arms. You can agree to disagree, you can return later and continue, or you can decide when it's time to end it. Establish this strategy BEFORE you go in. What are you willing to accept, what are you willing to give up in order to get what you want? What is going to determine when it has gone as far as it is going? How do you leave it?

Never let broken-off negotiations dangle. Make sure before you leave the room, there are specific, concrete decisions made. If you can't get them to commit to anything, get a concrete next step. If there is no 'next step', be prepared for what YOUR next step will be.

- Where do you walk to?

Are you going back to your desk or out the door? Are you going to pretend the discussion never took place, and it is business as usual? Do you plan to take it further? Is the horse truly dead, and you need to move on? Have you already figured out where you will move on to?

These must be established before you even *think* of negotiating, and before you hear your first 'no'. Be prepared for any one of the 'no's you may get. Just remember that it is only the starting point, the opening bid, the first volley.

Always keep in mind:

- Your Why
- The Math
- Your Self Worth

Let these 3 be your guardian angels whenever you ask for something you want. They will never let you down.

Lynda Hykin

9. WOMEN DON'T TAKE RISKS

A colleague introduced me to a gentleman that was looking to write his book and perhaps get into the speaking business. We met for coffee and talked about what each other was hoping to do. I wanted to be a speaker who writes, he wanted to be a writer that did speaker presentations. At the end of our conversation I hoped that I had inspired him to start working on his book and we went our separate ways.

About a month or so later I emailed him to see how he was coming along. Surprise, surprise! He had actually gone out, met some people, told them about his topic and the book he wanted to write, and suddenly found himself being booked (several times) *to speak*.

This was great and I was happy for him - except for the last line of his e-mail. "I guess I better put something together for a speech, because my first talk is next week". What??? I spent weeks and weeks (and sometimes months and months) going over my speeches, changing them, adding, deleting, making them perfect. Then they sit in my 'speeches' file until I pull them out again, and rework them some more.

This gentleman just 'throws together' a speech, and off he goes! The result? - Apparently he was a big hit! I was offended. Imagine, just throwing something together and then 'winging' it!

Of course once the indignity wore off, I was really happy for him. I took the lesson to heart. Men don't wait to be perfect before they do something. They go after something and tweak it as they go along. They just start. They go out there and DO something and work it until it gets good, then better and better the more they do it.

Women? Not so much.

Every day we take risks. Just stepping out the door can be a risk. Yet in the Working World, women often don't take risks. When it comes to our careers and what we want, we allow others to make those decisions for us. "If they thought I deserved the promotion, they would have offered it to me".

We tend to wait for recognition, for acknowledgement of our achievements. Even if we think we have earned the pay raise, promotion or opportunity to work on that huge, career-altering project, we wait. Surely, someone would have mentioned that I would be a good choice for this position, wouldn't they?

We feel we must have all our 'ducks in a row', conquer all possible objections, become 'perfect' before risking our current position. By the time all this has taken place, the opportunity has passed.

Men take risks all the time. If it doesn't work out, oh well. They don't take it as a personal reflection on themselves, but rather the circumstances surrounding the issue, they look at outside forces that caused the result.

Women take negative feedback personally. Women internalize it and do not look at outside forces. If they received a negative response, it's because *they* weren't good enough, or didn't deserve it, or weren't ready. We internalize negative feedback. Men externalize it. It was for reasons other than themselves that they did not get what they wanted therefore it is not a direct reflection on them personally.

For women, it's personal. Here are some reasons why:

- Women don't want to risk losing the relationship they have built with their coworkers, their colleagues and their boss.

- We don't want to risk being turned down, and being exposed to other's opinions.

- We don't want to risk losing more than what we already have.

- We don't want to risk having to prove ourselves again and again, or have to start over every time

Being informed, confident in yourself and knowing who you are will lessen the risk. Nothing is gained or achieved by not asking. You may not get everything you ask for 100% of the time, but you certainly will get nothing 100% of the time if you don't ask.

Challenge the Rules. Dreamers, Thinkers, Planners all challenge the rules. Just because "It has always been done this way" is no reason to continue to do it that way, if you have a better solution. In this new millennium, what worked 6 months ago could be outdated! The thing is, you are never going to get a home run or even get to first base if you don't step up to the plate and start swinging!

If you don't take that leap of faith, while you're busy making it 'perfect' someone else came up with the same idea, and ran with it, imperfections and all. It can be brainstormed, modified, adjusted later. Nothing is perfect the first time out.

We need to lighten up. Yes, be informed. Yes, have our data handy. Yes, know that it will work - as far as we know, with what information we have at the time. Then go do it. Get it out there! Take the personal out of it. Whatever you DO is never a reflection of who you ARE.

I had been writing this book for 3 years. It had to be perfect, because people were going to read it ... and in my mind, they were going to judge me (as a person) based on what I wrote. So I worked, and reworked the same chapters over and over. I worked them to death. It took so long that stats became outdated and I had to replace them. Meanwhile, other books started to appear. Yikes! Time to hustle and get it done!

And then I would work and rework the same chapters again and again, trying to make them perfect.

Then I had the enlightening 'aha' moment. My book is not who I **am**, it is simply information that I have researched and experienced and that I am sharing with others, that's it. Once this realization sunk in, I finished the book - in 6 weeks.

Here is another big reason women don't take risks. We don't get heard!

Make sure when you bring up an idea, suggestion or solution that you are HEARD! Repeat it until everyone has heard it. Many women sit in a meeting and wait for their turn to talk. We are very polite that way. We were taught not to interrupt. We also stop talking when someone interrupts us. (let`s play fair, everyone gets a turn talking….).

But we can never seem to get our turn back again. Men however, do not have this same compulsion for politeness. In their world, it is he who talks loudest and longest that wins! They interrupt at will. I love watching them; 2 men talking at the same time, oblivious to what the other one is saying – until one stands out as the dominant one. Then the other concedes (that is until the next opportunity).

I have literally had an idea that I put forth totally ignored, mostly because the guys were all talking at once. Thirty seconds later, someone else (male) said the exact same thing I had said, and everyone was astounded! What an amazing idea! Awesome dude! High five! I did not say anything. It would have seemed so petty to whine, stomp my feet and say, ``Hey, that was my idea!'' If I had made sure I got heard the first time, it wouldn't have eaten away at me…for weeks!

This is stand out, speak up time! Practice this because it is very important. If you have a total aversion to interrupting someone grab the first silent space, start talking and keep talking even if someone interrupts you (guaranteed, it will be a male). Sometimes women get a little aggressive. You'll hear them say – 'ya, but'… but then they stop and wait until you're finished. That is our little signal to say that we have something to say, so as soon as you're done it's my turn. Guys don't take turns. And most of the time even if they recognized your request to add to the conversation, they will keep right on talking.

It seems rude, and pushy. When two people are talking no one is listening. But you have to let them know you have something to say, something that can add value and that you deserve to be heard. If that means interrupting ... so be it.

Show them that you are not afraid to make your opinion known. One way is to ask their opinion about your idea. This grabs their attention. "What do you think about...?" You have now given them a problem to solve ... and given them your opinion. Some of you just started balking didn't you? Okay, could you simply stand up? I love doing this. If I'm sitting around the table with a group and I feel I'm not being heard, I simply stand up. The result is instant. Attention and focus is now on me. Simple and incredibly effective.

Sorry, ladies this one is a toughie... but you have to get heard to be heard. Practice helps.

At least until ...

Lynda Hykin

10. LACK OF MENTORSHIP AND ROLE MODELS

If you want to be successful, find someone who is already successful and do what they do. This is a Success Principle, written in almost every success and self-help book. It's good advice. Why struggle to re-invent the wheel?

- Who do you admire?

- Where are they?

- What do they do?

- Do you know them personally or do you look up to them from a distance?

- What qualities do they have that you want to replicate?

- Are there even any out there?

Only 29% of global Companies have any program for developing women in leadership roles and those programs vary in effectiveness. It looks like we are on our own!

Modeling after someone that has already made it to the top, close to the top, or has the lifestyle you want, can be like trying to find a needle in a haystack. They seem to be rare.

So where do you find them?

Start with your own Company. It doesn't have to be someone at a much higher level to want them as your mentor. It could be a colleague – she always seems to have it together, nothing frazzles her, she is as organized as a drill sergeant. She is assertive and feminine – all at the same time. She never has to yell but still makes her point. People listen to her. Seek out the women that you believe 'have it all together'. Look for someone you admire, that you would like to have the skills and leadership qualities that they possess. Do you and this person have the same belief systems, do you match when it comes to work ethic? Choose your mentor wisely. A mentor and mentee need to mesh, fit together. They should never be chosen for each other by someone else. They need to feel that each is a good match for the other. If you can't find someone within your Company, try an Organization or group you belong to, your bowling league, or a mom on the kid's baseball team.

Similar but different is sponsorship. This has much more commitment – on both sides. Both are held more accountable to each other. A good sponsor can help a woman's career sky rocket! A sponsor provides the 'networking' that most women miss out on. They provide introduction to key players and make them aware of juicy opportunities 'coming down the pipes'. You can benefit from a sponsor, but only if you are both totally committed to doing the work the sponsorship requires. She will train, encourage and hold you accountable to do the work. You will be truly committed to the sponsor to take her advice and do what she says to do. Trust that she knows what she is talking about. This is a totally win-win situation. You get the benefit of untold knowledge and experience, contacts that you may never have made on your own and it's fast tracked! The sponsor will benefit as well. They are seen as a visionary leader, someone who knows how to truly invest in their people. This will be a powerful and necessary talent in the years coming and those that are doing so will stand out far above the crowd. Do not under estimate what being a sponsor can do for you on a personal and profession level.

Here's another thing - it doesn't have to be a woman! Yes, a man that you admire, respect, and who is successful can be a sponsor to you. They can also bring the added bonus of seeing things 'from the other side'. This is an incredible opportunity for you to get perspective from both sides. Mind you, this would have to be a very enlightened leader to take our leadership style into consideration when they are mentoring you. Everyone wins – they get the reputation as an enlightened, forward thinking leader, and you get the training that can't be bought anywhere!

What if you can't think of anyone in your Company that you would want as a mentor or sponsor?

First, if this is your situation – I would seriously be thinking about why I want to be working there at all. You could go outside your Company, but be cautious – going to a mentor at the competitor's company is probably not a good idea. You don't want to be seen fraternizing with the enemy. Another company that is not considered a competitor is more logical. Again though, if there is no one in your Company I would seriously sit down to figure out why you would want to work there. Whose position are you aspiring to have? Is the reason you want it because you could do that job so much better? Good. Then go out and find someone who is already doing it better, and doing it the way you would if given the opportunity, even if it's a 'virtual' mentor.

I have several 'virtual mentors'. These are hugely successful women and men that I respect and admire – and have never met. I copy what they do, because they are doing it successfully. I manage myself and my business the way they do. Their beliefs and values match mine. This is a NON negotiable requirement for me when choosing a mentor or sponsor. If I don't believe what they stand for, their principles, and their morals, I don't care how successful they are, I will not model myself after them.

I can actually get more out of the 'virtual' mentor sometimes than a 'local' mentor. Don't get me wrong, both are great, but with the virtual mentor – you can have as many as you want and they can be as famous or rich or successful as you choose. I take a little of this from one, some of that from another – I choose the qualities that I like in each of them, and create – a brilliant and business savvy me! Still personal, still being myself - just doing things successfully!

A few books have hugely affected my life and set me on my journey to do what I do. One is "Making the Impossible Possible", by Bill Strickland. By the time I had read up to page 58, I had cried 3 times. I remember it was a Sunday and I hopped on the computer, looked him up and emailed him. I told him I wanted to do what he was doing. I explain how even though I hadn't finished reading the book yet, he had made a huge impact on my life. He emailed me back and said, "Come to Pittsburgh and see what we do." He gave me a contact name to let them know when I could come so they could show me around and just like that, I was invited to go to Pittsburgh, meet with him and see what he does! He went from being a just an author of a book I was reading to a 'virtual' mentor, to someone I actually knew!

When I wanted to research 100 wise women, I found a website with that name. It was a fantastic organization – from Kentucky. Again, I emailed one of the ladies on the website, asking if she could give me any information about their organization because I would love to start something similar in Canada. Voila! Not only was she ready to give me everything I needed to know to start an organization such as theirs, but she invited me to come and sit at one of their meetings, and then we would spend the day going over how to make this happen here in Canada. (ya gotta love the internet). Another mentor – without ever knowing them or being introduced by someone else! It can be that easy.

As the sponsored or mentored one, you need to prove yourself worthy of sponsorship. So, we are kind of back at square one – you have to let others know what you are doing, working on, and where you want to go so that a sponsor can help you get there. Being totally committed to yourself, and your career is a start. If self promoting feels bad for you, this can be a blessing for you. This is a way around it. Someone else – your sponsor - can toot your horn for you, praise your talents and skills.

The best part is that sponsorship can be done at any level, whether you are fresh out of college and starting your first real career position or you want to get into the fast-lane and fly! Perhaps you have been home raising your children and now want back into the Working World. A sponsor who recognizes your talent can take you further and faster than trying to make it on your own.

Whether you are being sponsored or mentored, or whether you are helping someone else, everyone benefits. Making an impact can be as easy as helping one woman change her life, simply by encouraging her to recognize and expand her talents. Taking your career to the next level, or putting it on the fast track, can be as simple as … wait for it … asking!

Lynda Hykin

JOURNAL ENTRY 4

Taking each of my Top Ten Reasons, answer the following questions:

1. Fear
   - What are you afraid of when it comes to asking for what you want?
   - List all of them
   - Ask yourself "What if" and then write down 5 positive possible outcomes to that fear. For example; I'm afraid my boss will say no when I ask for a raise. Then do this: 'What if' I asked for $2.00 raise, and the boss said I really deserve $5.00? 'What if' he gives me a promotion that comes with an even bigger raise – and a car allowance? 'What if' he offers me the opening in Hawaii – with a huge living allowance? Get crazy with this. Think totally outside the box.
   - How does it feel to think about these positive possibilities?

2. What **you** believe you're worth
   - Do you value yourself and your work?
   - Assess your skills.
   - Write down everything you do well that you *know* you are good at.
   - Write down what other people say you are good at.
   - Write down everything you love about your current and past jobs
   - Write down everything you dislike about your current and past jobs
   - Choose one to three things that you will stop doing beginning today, that you dislike
   - Choose one to three things that you want to keep doing, that you like and will learn to do better
   - Share it with your boss. Put a plan together to do more of what you like and lose or do less of what you don`t

When you love what you do, you strive to be really good at it. Your boss would love you to be great at what you do…so tell them what it is and ask to do more of that!

3. Gender Differences
    • When you are out at the mall or shopping watch people, how they talk, interact, stand, sit with each other, in groups and even by themselves.
    • In restaurants notice how couples sit, how their body language shows what they are thinking, how comfortable they look.
    • Practice on someone from the opposite sex. Make them feel comfortable. Stand, approach them and talk to them in a way that will make them more receptive to you and what you are saying
    • What happened?
    • Did you notice a difference in their responsiveness toward you?

4. Good Girl Syndrome
    • Write down every time you catch yourself saying yes when you want to say no, for a week.
    • The next week try saying no when someone asks you to do something you really don't want to do.
    • What happened both times?
    • How did you feel?
    • Do you notice any difference in how they interact with you now?

5. Low Expectations – Self Discrimination
    • Track how many times you promote someone else.
    • Have you ever secretly wanted something for yourself, but gave it away?
    • Why did you do that?
    • How did you feel?
    • Congratulate yourself out loud when you do something good, or achieve a goal or solve a problem. Repeat it at least three times during the day. It can be as simple as "Yes! I rock!" or "Yes! I

did it, awesome me!" If someone asks what you're doing – tell them. I just did ….

- How do you feel when you congratulate yourself?

6. Achievements
    - List your greatest achievements
    - Then tell someone
    - List the things you want from your job or position
    - Then tell someone
    - List where you want to take your career in the next year, then in the next 5 years
    - Now take all of that and go tell your boss

7. Work-Life Balance
    - Write down your ideal job
    - Write down your ideal life
    - If you have family, ask them to write down their ideal life with you
    - Compare lists
    - Does your family want the same things you do or is their list totally different?
    - Together, can you come up with a satisfactory list that would make everyone happy?
    - List as many ideas that just pop into your head about how you can make your job and your career work together? Get as crazy as you can.
    - What would need to happen to make the ideal life/work balance a reality?

8. The Word 'No'
    - Do you believe the word no means you are not worthy?
    - What does the word 'no' mean to you?
    - How do you feel when someone tells you 'no' when you ask for something?

- Can you remember a time when 'no' did NOT affect or bother you?
- Why didn't it bother you?
- Did you feel empowered?
- What did you do?
- Practice hearing the word no as an incentive to ask more questions, to dig deeper to find out EXACTLY what they mean

9. Taking Risks
   - Do you take risks?
   - What would you take even a small risk for?
   - What makes it worth taking that risk?
   - What result would you expect to receive from taking that risk?
   - Write it down, starting with "I could see myself ….." (doing this, asking for that, trying something new). Remember, this doesn't have to be just about money, this is also about your career and your life. Then write down the reward for doing it.
   - If you come up against a negative barrier or a fear, play - What if? Simply write down your barrier. Then say "what if …… and make it a positive solution. For example. I'm afraid if I ask my boss for a raise, he'll fire me. Now 'what if…..' What if he says yes? What if he gives me MORE than I asked for? What if he offers me a chance to work on that new project? What if…..
   - Now, how do you feel?
   - If a situation arises and you have to choose between two options, choose the one that you wouldn't normally choose.
   - Try it, just once
   - What happened?
   - If you are really timid, start with something small – like ordering the same old thing in the restaurant – try something you have never tried before. If you like it, you found a new dish and if you didn't, well, you know that you can actually say, "At least I tried it"! If this one is really scary – ask the server what they recommend as the best. If you like it … big tip. If you don't

like it, let them know! And still big tip, after all you are a generous person and are going to have a lot more money than before!

10. Lack of Mentor/ Role Model

- Who was your idol or your hero when you were growing up?
- What was it that you liked/idolized/ about them?
- Are they still your hero?
- If your hero/idol has changed and you have someone new, do they have different qualities than the one before?
- Did they change or did you?
- Why?
- What qualities do you admire in others?
- Are they the same qualities you admire in yourself? (ooh, betcha' didn't see that coming!)
- If you had a mentor or sponsor, what would you want them to help you with?
- If someone asked you to mentor them, would you?

Lynda Hykin

"Life is no longer out of my control.

It is exactly how I want it to be."

- Lynda Hykin

Lynda Hykin

PART THREE

MASTERY

IF YOU DON'T CONTROL YOUR LIFE,

SOMEONE ELSE WILL

AKA

THE HOW

Lynda Hykin

INTRODUCTION

Yes, here it is, the HOW! Finally, what you have been waiting for this entire time!

You have made it. You know what you want. You know your why. You have identified the barriers that are causing you to not ask for what you want. You have answered the questions in your journal.

You are on that road to success!

Part One Motivation - complete

Part Two Momentum - complete

Bravo!

See, it wasn't so bad was it? You are so much wiser now. Even if you never read any further, (as if I could stop you) you could go out and change how you see the Working World, how you see your business or career. By implementing what you have learned so far, you may create a better life for yourself.

Before reading any further remember that we are dealing with human beings, with emotions, perceptions and beliefs that are unique to each of us. Only you know you best. Only you know what feels right for you. Always hold on to who you are, your beliefs and your values and take them with you everywhere, and into every negotiation. This is your world and it is up to you to create the world you want. You get to decide what works best for you, which situations and scenarios would be most applicable to your situation. How you do anything is how you do everything.

You get to negotiate as a woman – valuable, knowledgeable, skilled, and worthy. You can walk into any room, anywhere, any situation, and know that you deserve what you want.

Here we go – The time has come. What you have been waiting for has arrived. Here are specific steps, hints and tips on how to do that…

THE NEGOTIATION PROCESS

CHAPTER 1

THE PLAN

I have broken the process down into two main strategies for negotiating:

- The Plan

- The Delivery

The Plan

You need to gather the information that is:

- Relevant to the meeting BEFORE the meeting

- About the person you will be negotiating with

- Their Title and position

- Their working relationship to you if any

- Their personality, values, beliefs, habits, quirks, likes, dislikes – if possible. This obviously isn't relevant if you are talking to a stranger over the phone. But you can tell their mood by their voice, how they are treating you and what they are saying. Listen for clues.

- The point you are going to be negotiating; it's benefits/the problem it solves/the benefit to the company/to the person you are presenting it to/how it is a win-win solution

- Their possible objections – anticipate what they may say and have a solution to that ready

- Your current physical/mental/emotional state and theirs. If you are feeling sick, have a headache, tired, or stressed from personal issues, don't start. The same for the other party. If they are not feeling well, it will not be the best time. Reschedule.

Timing

- Negotiate BEFORE you accept a position

- Ask, when YOU are ready and prepared

- Ask when you know they are more receptive.

- The mood of the participants

After a big argument with another employee or having just been dressed down by their own boss? Not a good time. As they are running out the door to catch a flight or get to a meeting? Not a good time. Asking for a substantial raise when your boss just got back from the divorce lawyer? Perhaps not the best timing.

If everyone is looking for a fight or hard time, that's exactly what will happen. If the air is filled with apprehension and mistrust, try and soothe the energy. Ease into the session, make others feel comfortable… yes this is okay to do. You are not succumbing to the stereo-type or lowering your standards. Remember to choose your battles. Offering a nice warm cup of tea when they looked totally stressed? If it gets them to relax and appreciate the gesture, it is more likely to get you what you are there to accomplish. Or, have your assistant get it for them. Even better! Makes you the authority figure… nice…..

Did you know that a man's testosterone level fluctuates at certain times of the day? Yep! Early in the morning it is like a hole in the dyke! They ooze testosterone in the morning, making them 'somewhat' more aggressive. Is this the best time to ask for something? Perhaps not. This level increases again in the early evening. The best time to catch them in a more mellow mood? You guessed it! Right after lunch! Lower testosterone and a full belly – works for me!

Location

Try to set the meeting up in your domain. This gives you the psychological 'home turf' advantage. If it is in their office, try to avoid being in the 'interviewee' seat. Suggest sitting at a table or where all parties are at least at 'equal' seating. This sometimes isn't possible. If nothing else, move your chair so that you are not facing them directly. Put it on an angle. If it is in neutral territory or there is more than one person at the meeting, get there early and have only one chair at the head of the table – yours. Of course, if someone else called the meeting, relinquish this to them. You don't want to start off on the wrong foot by insulting them and taking their status away.

BATNA

Remember, it means the Best Alternative To a Negotiated Agreement – aka the Back-up Plan

- Know what your alternative action steps are, for both success and if things don't go as planned

- Expect counter offers and flat out 'no's and have alternatives ready

Smaller companies may be more flexible than larger or unionized companies – so you may have to get 'creative' dealing with the bigger boys. Total compensation rather than just one item may work better. Instead of just, 'I want '$ XXXX.00', you can include money, more on your expense allowance, travel, etc. as a total package. Always have bargaining chips that you don't care about letting go of in order to gain what you really want.

Negotiating is about give and take. You can't have it all your way (all the time) so you want to be able to 'give' them something in exchange for something you want. Make sure that although it doesn't mean much to you, it has meaning to them. Otherwise, it's a useless chip.

- Do you leave? Do you stay? Do you know?

Make sure you know what you are going to BEFORE going in. NEVER let them know what that is. Saying something like, "I want a 50% raise, or I quit" may just get you shown the door, and there is no way you can back down from a statement like that.

Leverage

- Know what they need

- Know what the solution to their problem is

- Offer the solution making it unique to you

- Let them know you have/are the best – and you are willing to offer it to them for what you believe it's worth. If they want it, they will pay what it is worth. What it is worth is what you decide it is worth. After all, it's yours – you have the solution! When you walk into a store, there is a price on an item. The store has decided this is what they want for that item, why can't we do the same thing?

- Your workload is excellent leverage – especially if you are performing far above and beyond the current job description

- You have something they want – and they have something you want. If your 'something' is worth more to them than their 'something' is to you – well, there you go-leverage!

Best for All

- Remember it is a two way process where BOTH parties walk away feeling good about receiving the maximum benefit.

- Know that you are doing this to benefit everyone. This will make you more comfortable going in. Your goal is not to strip them naked. You want to make sure they get something too (that's the nurture thing popping up) which can make you more controlled and empowered.

- Look at it like you are doing them a favor, because you are!

Solutions

- Always have more than one solution or alternative to their possible or probable objectives

- Ask, "What do you think is fair?" "How do you think we can resolve this" Asking someone's opinion always works to your advantage. You're letting them know you want to solve this and their input, advice or suggestions are valued. Just watch out for the head nodding!

Step outside the Box

- They said no to money - What about benefits, time off, working from home, 4 10 hour days?

- Give up certain benefits that you are not using for more of one that you do use. For example – you get an amount for glasses, but you don't wear glasses, can that money be allocated somewhere else?

I actually negotiated for this. We received a $400 yearly fitness allowance. It could be used for any fitness activity; gym membership, golf, hockey, anything that meant physical fitness. I asked to be reimbursed for my gardening supplies. They said no. I asked if they had ever spent the day gardening, bending, crouching, hauling dirt, shoveling gravel, lifting patio stones - or did they use their money so they could ride the 9 holes in a golf cart? I got the $400. NOTE: This became a standard for anyone in the entire Company that wanted to use it for gardening.

Network

- This is HUGE! Network, network, network. Talk to people, get your name and face and personality out there!

- Make the time. There is no way around this one. Once a month, once a week – make it your commitment. Being out of the loop is being out of the running and out of the money.

- If you absolutely can't be out there, find out who is and ask them to keep you in touch with what is happening, who are the movers and shakers. This would be where a mentor or sponsor would be a great benefit.

I used to be proud of the fact that I never listened to gossip, to conversations around the break room or at various social functions. This meant I was also the last to know when something was happening. Everyone seemed to know before me! Gossip is one thing, especially listening to or spreading rumors and spiteful or hurtful comments. There is a difference between listening to gossip, and listening to real things that are happening. The break room is a great place to find out if someone's leaving, getting promoted, or moving to a different department. If you hear of anything like this always make sure you go right to the **source** to **verify** the information first before you take any action. Otherwise, it could be very embarrassing!

- If you freeze up talking to people you don't know – take courses, join a club like Toastmasters or find networking groups. This is probably the most effective way to find out what`s going on, who is the 'go to' person, what companies are doing, and what they are paying. It's also a great opportunity to find out about opportunities in other companies and businesses.

Find a Mentor/Sponsor

- This can be done in one of the above avenues or in your workplace.

  - If you are in business for yourself, other women entrepreneurs are great places to look for mentors.

  - Check out newspaper articles on successful women, then check them out on the internet. If you like what you see, email them or phone them, tell them who you are and what you are looking for. I have almost always gotten a reply from anyone that I have contacted – and usually directly from them, not just their assistant!

Barbara Stanny is one of my 'virtual mentors'. Just by following what she does and how she conducts business improves my abilities. How about Oprah – if you ran your business like she runs hers or used the techniques she uses in your job, would you be more successful? – you bet you would. And you didn't have to know her personally to do it!

No matter what plan you come up with, have a plan. It's like starting a business and needing to obtain funding. You can't just walk into the bank and ask for a couple hundred thousand dollars and expect them to hand it over. They require a plan to see how you are going to pay it back. You need a plan to know what you are going to do – if you are successful – and if you are not. Just remember, it does NOT have to be perfect! Just know your stuff and then share it!

Lynda Hykin

CHAPTER 2

THE DELIVERY

"Let's split the difference"

Be very aware of this seemly simple solution if you are heading toward a stalemate situation. If you are negotiating, giving and taking and then it seem to stall, and they suggest splitting the difference, it may sound good but watch:

You start at   10,000

They counter at   6,000

You come back at   9,000

They say let's split the difference (9,000-6,000) 3,000 difference – each will 'give up 1,500.

For you that means 9,000-1500= 7,500

For them it means   6,000+1500= 7,500

Remember you started at 10,000 and end up with 7,500 the actual difference is $2,500 less.

They started at 6,000 and end up at 7,500 the difference is only $1,500 more.

Always go back to the original offer, which is your 10,000 to their 6,000. Split *that* difference.

The difference is 4,000. You give up $2,000 and they gave up $2,000. You would have lost $500.00 just by not going back to the original offer. That $500 might not seem like a lot, but … yep, do the math over the course of your career; including your pension, your benefits, and everything else your base salary is used to calculate, not to mention the interest on that money over 20 years.

Beware of Dead Air!

This is number one on the practice list. Present your offer, and then be quiet! Sorry, but diving in to explain all the reasons why you should, could, would and must have this actually weakens your position.

- What if they agree! What if they offer you more! What a waste of verbal time if that should happen. Of course, if they do, then perhaps you didn't set the bar high enough, which will be your lesson for the next time.

- Secondly, it gives them time to absorb what you just asked for and how they are going to counter. By not saying anything, it makes you appear more in control of what you want.

- Do not immediately jump in to fill the space! When they are quiet, it could be just because they are thinking, but most likely it's because they know most people feel the need to fill the gap and keep the conversation going even if it means rambling. In a negotiation this causes a tendency to start backing down, and can eventually have you backing yourself right out of anything. Think "Silence is Consent", instead of "Silence means No".

Crying Wolf

Have you ever heard a child (or for that matter an adult) continuously whine and repeatedly ask for a multitude of things? "I want, I want, I want…." Eventually you tune them out. Their 'wants' do not seem important because they want EVERY thing. Choose wisely what you ask for. Repeatedly going back and asking for more and more and more makes what you ask for less and less valuable. Constantly wanting is counter-productive, which is why we do our homework first. A list of 5 things – giving up 3 to get 2 – that's okay. Going in with a list of 20 – giving up 2 – not so much. Then going back in two weeks later with another list of 20 – career suicide!

Be prepared to give up something of perceived value in order to get what you REALLY want. It may appear to them to be worth something to you, but you know that it doesn't, or that it is not worth as much as they believe it to be.

Be Assertive, not Aggressive

- Men will demand this and that. Pound on the tables and let the spit fly! Women – well, not lovin' the idea too much! Negotiating like a man does not work for women. We don't like it and men don`t like it. Being assertive is much more our style. I love that commercial for a yogurt - she says, 'please take my clothes in, I`ve been eating key lime pie, strawberry cheesecake' and the tailor says, 'you mean let them out'. She very politely says no, 'in', and just keeps politely repeating it over and over. The tailor is having a hard time trying to argue with her because she is not rising to the bait, just simply stating what she wants – take the clothes 'in'. That's assertive. Get your point across without all the drama.

- Always try to keep your emotions outside the room. There is no place for them in a negotiation. I know that it's really hard to do if things start to get out of control, but it just weakens your position. If you feel them bubbling up and are afraid they will spill over, look at your watch and say let's take a 5 minute break. Then leave and head for the washroom. Some deep breathing, cold water, kicking the garbage can, whatever it takes, get it out and then go back in.

I know this sound ominous and melodramatic, but when something is SO important to you, the emotions attached to it can get in the way. Even if you are going crazy on the inside don't let it be visible on the outside.

Fake it until you make it

Yecht! This is a 'what **NOT**' to do. I HATE this expression! Yet, this is how a lot of men operate. They say yes I can do that, they are given the opportunity and THEN they go away and try to figure out how. We women decide first whether we can or can't and *then* ask for the opportunity.

You have already figured out your worth and your value so this statement no longer applies. You do not have to fake it. You know you can do it. Just because you haven't done it before does not mean you don't have the skills or the capability. Go for it! ('Take a calculated risk' I believe applies here.) Listen to others when they say you can do it; sometimes they are more objective and less critical of you than you are. The only failure is the one when you didn't even attempt something. I tried at having a retail business – twice.

Did I fail? Not at all – because I DID it! And I learned that I don't like running a retail business! Two success stories in my books!

CHAPTER 3

THE INTERVIEW

Note: These are not just for interviews. They are steps you can use *whenever* you are negotiating, whether it's your first job or you've been with the Company for 10 years.

The First Interview

Always remember you are there because you are the best candidate to solve their problem. Remember that they have a problem and YOU are the solution!

You are a business woman, not just a prospective employee.

- Hand them your business card just after you shake their hand. You made business cards, right? There is no reason not to have a card. You can now get 500 color business cards made up for under $25. This immediately puts you on a more business-oriented and unique level than any other candidate. This tells them that you believe yourself to be a professional, and deserving of respect. It is also a huge boost to your self confidence! They don't have to be fancy, just make sure they have:

- Your name – Highlighted and bigger than the rest of the text on the card

- Your title – such as Professional Administrative Assistant, Professional Receptionist, whatever business you are in. If you stock shelves for a living – your Title can be 'Inventory

Management Professional'. Doesn't that sound and look better than 'stocked shelves' on your resume?

- Current contact info – Do NOT cross out old phone numbers or email and write a new one in pen – it looks unprofessional and tacky, not the first impression you want to make.

- Your email on a professional card should also be professional. Having an email like 'hotbabe23@yippykaiyaye.com' is probably not something the prospective employer will want to have to reply to – and most likely won`t.

- Optional is a **professional** picture of you. An amateurish web cam photo will psychologically reflect on you and your qualities. Use a professional photo or leave it off your card.

- Dress appropriately for the position. Depending on the business you are applying for - flash and dazzle is good for film industry, not so good for an accountant. Psychologically, they want people just like themselves. Yes I know you want to be free to be yourself. You also want the job. There are times to exercise your freedom of expression but your first interview may not be one of them. (However, you do have the power to make your own choices.)

- Like the Girl Guide motto, Be Prepared. Always bring an extra copy of your **most recent** resume.

- Anticipate their needs – your diplomas (already copied for them) and anything else in your portfolio; accomplishments, courses taken, volunteer work.

- Have written referrals and recommendations attached to your resume. This saves them time, and you look organized and prepared.

- When they ask if you have any questions, have some! They can be as simple as, "Where do you see the Company going over the next few years in terms of growth?" If you have researched the Company beforehand, you know their mission statement, their vision and their philosophy. Asking questions around these can show that you actually did check them out – you did your homework. Points! Okay, so that takes care of the interview, but what does this have to do with negotiating in the interview? Well, all this has built your confidence up and prepared you for the next part of the interview, which is … the money part!

Most Companies advertise a salary or wage range in the ad when recruiting. In the interview they may ask what you are looking for in a salary. **Avoid** this question if at all possible! You want them to make the first offer and this usually is not done until the final interview or a job offer is on the table.

If you must answer, make statements similar to the following:

- I noticed your ad stated $xxx per hour. That may be within my range, but I will need more information.
- We can talk about that later in the process
- Those figures are something we can work with
- I am open to discussing that when there is an offer

If they say flat out they are not going above what was advertised, say that you are still interested in the position and would like to go further into the process before making a decision.

- If they are adamant amount a figure, give them what you already planned on starting with before you went into the interview.

- If they ask what you were making at your last position, try not to give them an exact figure but NEVER lie about it. A quick call to your former employer for the answer and you will be out the door before you even got in. You can say that what you made before wouldn't be relevant because the job descriptions are different, and you have gained a lot more experience and skills during your employment at your last position. Perhaps the salary was the reason for leaving the other Company. This is good information to give them. It shows that you stand by your commitment to yourself.

- Ask what is next in the hiring process before negotiating any salary. If there will be a 2nd interview, hold off any discussions until then. Simply say that you would like to discuss that when you are further into the hiring process.

Here are a couple examples of why you should wait to disclose any salary during the 1st interview:

1. I applied for a position with a company that had a salary range of $24,000-$26,000. I decided I was going to ask for the top, $26,000. I didn't think about setting a figure higher than that, because that was what I actually wanted. I didn't think about having some 'wiggle' room. I thought the wiggle would come when I asked for the $26,000. I also thought $26,000 was as high as they would go, because that was the top of their salary range. They offered me $26,000 right at the start! I got so excited about getting what I wanted, that I didn't think to negotiate for more. I also didn't have the job explained in more detail. Two BIG mistakes! The job that they advertised and the actual work that I was expected to perform were two VERY different things. I also found out that benefits didn't kick in until you had been there a year, and then they were poor compensation. Oh wait, three mistakes! Once I was working, I discovered lunch breaks were 'frowned upon' and you were expected to work for 9 hours, not 8, which brought the actual rate much lower than I thought I was getting! I should have taken a risk and started *outside* the high range, or asked more questions about the job before I accepted their offer.

2. Another interview I had went the *other* way. Really listen to what they are saying about the job and what their expectations are. Let them talk as much as they want. They will disclose some golden nuggets that you can use to your benefit. Listen carefully and you will most likely discover some beautiful

`bargaining chips`. The salary advertised was maximum $2,600 per month. I was really good at what I did and knew what I could get for my skills in the market. I also knew the employer had a reputation of being 'high maintenance'. I went in with the expectation of the top of the range being my bottom line. The interviewer – who was also the boss, loved to talk and I let him. The more he talked about his vision of my role and my position in the Company, the higher I mentally raised my rate. When he was done and asked what I was looking for in a salary, I told him - $3500 per month to start and reviewed in 3 months with an opportunity to make a commission. He gulped – and accepted it. He should have quit talking!

Lynda Hykin

CHAPTER 4

2nd INTERVIEW or

THE JOB OFFER

- Get all offers in writing so there are no misunderstandings. If they are adamant about it being their final offer, and some are, ask for time to make a decision. Brow beating, demanding a now or never decision immediately could be a sign that perhaps this is not the right company for you to be working for.

- You want to compare with the other offers you have received before making a final decision. The more job offers you have on the table, the easier it is for you to negotiate without the desperation of accepting anything that comes along. Don't lie about other offers – make sure you have one.

- Once salary has been discussed (not necessarily agreed to – yet) you can now bring up questions such as probationary period, any benefits, stocks, pension – most will explain these in advance, but if they don't, ASK! Questions like:

- When do they take effect

- What is the % paid by Company. Some 'benefits' are mandatory – by the employee. Stock contributions can be one of these, contributions to a pension plan and RRSPs can be another. Union dues will be deducted if you decide to opt in, so make sure you find out if and how much. It really sucks on your first pay, when there is over $300 in deductions that you didn't realize you had to pay for!

- Can you make contributions to pension or company stock through payroll? Does the Company contribute or have a match program?

I can feel you seizing up already! I know what you're saying to yourself or thinking… Wait until I got the job, I can ask all this stuff after! NO, no, no! Ask **before** you sign on the dotted line! It's okay, it is considered appropriate at this time. It also makes you look like a responsible, savvy business person, who does their due diligence. You will not seem greedy, or only out for what's in it for you (I used to think like this). These are legitimate questions that you are entitled to ask. You are simply clarifying so that there are no misunderstandings later. If it makes you feel better, you can even say … so to get a clear picture of everything the company has to offer …"

You need to know everything the Company is offering, or not offering because you want to assign a dollar value to it.

- Take notes during the negotiation stage. Write down verbal agreements in case it is 'missing' from the written offer.

- If it is a very small Company with less than 35 employees, most likely there will be no benefits or Company contributions. This is important to know before you are hired because you still need dental and medical services. If you have to pay out of pocket for these you need to add it into what you want for your wage so that these expenses are covered.

- Know the hours you will be working.

I took a full time position for $18/hr. which I thought was better than a $16/hr position – no brainer, do the math, right? $2/hr more!

Except… it wasn't. The $18/hr was for 7 hours per day, plus a ½ hour unpaid lunch. The $16/hr position was for 8 hours per day, with a paid lunch. $18/hr for 35 hours - $630 per week; $16/hr for 40 hours - $640 per week -$40/month more! You incur the same day to day expenses (bus fare, gas, lunch etc), it's only ½ hr. difference in total time, but at the end of a year – you made $480 more at the rate of $16/hr. Remember, this also affects your pension etc.

- How long is the probationary period? Is salary reviewed at that time? Although 3 months seems to be the norm, I have had it as long as 4 months, 6 months, even a year.

- What is involved in the probationary period and what are their expectations of your performance?

- How long before the benefits become effective? This is important. Some companies start on your actual Anniversary date, some the 1st of the month following your start date. Yanking out all your teeth because you now have benefits only to find out they don't kick in until the beginning of the next month can be very costly – for you!

Remember, when an interviewer chooses you, they are also making this decision because they have to look good to their boss. They need to score the best candidate. They are the experts in the company at choosing new employees. If you perform well, you make them look good to their boss and their peers. If you don't, they look bad. So they have a vested interest in you being the best!

Your worth is reflected in your salary. The more you get paid, the greater your skills and experience are worth. They get to brag that they got the best – and your salary should prove it. Remember you are there because you are the best candidate out of hundreds or even thousands that applied. You can solve their problems; you have something valuable the Company wants.

- Something doesn't feel right? Ask now or forever hold your peace. They can't offer more than what that position's grade is? Perhaps then you should be starting at the next grade.

- When the interview is finished and you have asked all the questions you need to and you have the information to make a decision, ask the interviewer when they need an answer. Try not to accept their offer until you have had time to make sure you are not forgetting anything – that could prove vital a few months down the road, if you have this opportunity. I know it seldom happens any more, where you make them wait for a decision, rather than the other way around. In today`s world this doesn`t happen too often. Reality is that there are only a few jobs and a few thousand applying. If you REALLY want the job, and all the answers are acceptable to you, you may accept the offer. Just make sure that your contract can be reviewed 3 months down the road. If you made a mistake somewhere, you will only have to bear it for a short period.

They will most likely tell **you** when **they** will make a decision – by Friday, by next week etc. Ask them to contact you whether you have the position or not, you don't want to be left hanging and will need to move forward with other options. I have noticed that if you got the position, they phone you first, so an early call is a good indication.

If you find the waiting period excessively long, mention it. "I would like to move forward with other interviews if I am not selected for this position. Is it possible to give me some indication or make the decision sooner?" I have waited and waited, called, followed up, spent lots of wasted time without getting an answer. Finally, I said that I needed an answer by Thursday, or I would move on. I moved on. Turns out they weren't prepared to hire anyone, they were just fishing. It was two weeks wasted. Well, not entirely because I learned not to wait – to follow up and then move on.

Always remember that not only are you being interviewed, but you are interviewing the Company. Unless you enjoy job hopping, or temporary assignments, you want to feel good about where you are working, what you are doing, and what you are being paid to do. As hard as it is to refuse a job when you are tired of looking, and jobs are scarce, the stress of working somewhere where you are not happy, or doing a job you hate, will have you quitting or worse, not quitting thereby doing you and the Company no favors. The right job is out there for you. You'll know it when it arrives. Take your time to find it. Besides, you have your 'sleep at night' fund to cover you until it comes (just checking).

You got the Job!

I have actually worked for Companies that frowned on taking a lunch – one went so far as to say "you don't get a lunch" (and you get to work 10 or 12 hrs. per day for 8 hours of pay, gee thanks) This is illegal. I don't recommend reciting passages from the Human Rights Code, but take your lunch. If someone questions it, simply tell them you are taking a lunch, you are much more effective at your job when you do. You do not need to explain any further to anyone.

You also need to take periodic breaks if you sit all day, for health reasons! Make sure you actually get up, and get away from your desk. My lunch used to be checking emails and answering phone messages while scarfing down whatever food happened to be in front of me. Trust me when I say you will not get a pat on the back for doing it so don't look for one. You will also not be able to use that when negotiating in the future… "I never take a lunch, I come in early, stay late…" I can hear the boss now: "No-one asked you to do that, although I do appreciate your willingness to do so." Translation: what a good girl!

Or it backfires: Obviously you need extra time to do your current job, so how will you manage to take on even more responsibility with the promotion you want?

Your Career

The above tips aren't just for an interview. Think about what you want. If any of the above seem like something you want that you are not getting from your current position, perhaps it's time to ask for it.

Here are some more things to think about negotiating for:

- Do they offer, or would they consider (Oh look, a bargaining chip!) tuition assistance to improve your skills and bring more benefit to the position and Company?

- Will you be able to attend conferences, seminars, company Trade Shows (if you see this as a benefit to move up the ladder)?

- Very few Companies offer sick time in today's Working World. If you are sick and don't get paid for it… do the math… add it into your compensation package. Calculate 1 day per month and add it to the annual salary.

Your Time

Can you:

- work from home one or more days a week

- Job share

- Work 4-10 hour days instead of 5-8 hour

- Vacation schedule – can you get more vacation in lieu of a dollar amount?

- Paid/Unpaid leave of absence

Signing Bonus.

This one is overlooked quite often. This is a one-time offer of money and can be used in the negotiation process as an incentive for you to accept the position.

Several years ago this was huge in the United States and in rural areas of Canada. Desperately seeking qualified nursing staff and doctors they offered incredible signing bonuses to graduates just for accepting a job offer with them. Use caution with any signing bonus because it will not be reflected in your base salary; and that is what everything else will be based on – annual increases, pension etc. Those who offer this are usually pretty savvy with how it can be manipulated to look great on paper – and not so great in the bank account.

Again, use your mantra here: a $10,000 signing bonus over a period of a 20 year career – works out to $41.67 per year. (quick math, without interest etc.) It would be much more to your advantage to 'relinquish' the signing bonus for $1,000 per year added to your base wage. $1,000 per year for 20 years, again quick math without interest etc. - $20,000 – much better! The advantage of a signing bonus is that you get it immediately (make sure you do, and not in payments over a period of time; this is your career not a hockey contract – unless of course it is a… never mind, just get it up front in one lump sum!)

Always, always, always, (I hope I am clear on this) ALWAYS ask for the shortest probation period possible (in writing please) that your salary can be reviewed - without a *specific, pre-determined* amount of increase. Should you determine the position is much more involved or you have a lot more responsibilities that you weren't told about, or tasks were added after you started your original position, and you agreed to a $1 per hour raise when you signed – well you can see how this is not good. Leaving it open will give you wiggle room to renegotiate and allow you to determine your new worth – and how you should be compensated for the work you are actually performing. By this time you have a good feel for what you are contributing and know your value (right?) If that makes you nervous, add a dollar figure that has a range – and make it a handsome range; "after 3 months, wage will be increased between $ and $, depending on the responsibilities of the position at that time". This gives you two things; a little more leverage, and a negotiation opportunity! Perhaps you can take the lower end of the range, and add an extra day off, etc. See! Automatic negotiating opportunity! (**now you got it!**)

This also works for an annual review. Negotiate whenever you have the opportunity. It is never just a one-time thing. It is ever evolving, always ongoing, just like your career and your life. I refused a position once because they wanted a 6 month probation period. That's too long to go without at least a review. We negotiated and agreed to a 6 month probation period, with my salary reviewed after 3 months. I got a $1.50 per hour increase at the 3 month mark, and then another $2 at the 6 month mark THEN at the 6 month mark I renegotiated for a new contract!

Whether it's the first or final interview or your yearly review, it's an opportunity to reflect on everything you have accomplished in your role, what you have brought to the Company, your successes and the improvements you have made. You change and grow continuously, so should your career and your pay-check. Even if you are an entrepreneur, you need to give **yourself** a review every 3 or 6 months and then an annual one. Ask the same questions, look at the same strategies to see where you can ask for what you want, where you can negotiate to get something - for your 'why'. See how much you have grown and then get paid for where you are now, not where you were. You now have more skills, more experience and more qualities that need to be reassessed and recognized – and paid for.

JOURNAL ENTRY 5

Practice

Go out and negotiate for something small, something that you really don't care whether or not you get. Cell phone and cable companies are great places to start. Get two or three 'plans' from different companies, compare them and then start negotiating. These are great businesses to practice with because it's impersonal. You don't see the other person face-to-face and you have nothing invested in their company personally.

Negotiating is addicting! Once you get that sense of empowerment, you *own* your self confidence. You will really begin to see what is out there, just waiting for you to ask for!

- Day care - take one child, get a discount on the second child, car maintenance and services

- You could offer referrals in exchange for a discount – a great bargaining chip! ("I know people")

- Insurance companies

These are all excellent places to start. When you're ready to hit up the boss, practice first with someone you trust, preferably someone who knows the person you will be negotiating with. Choose someone who can anticipate the objections the other person may come up with.

- Were you successful?

- How did you feel

    o Before you started

    o While you were negotiating

    o After the negotiation

o If you weren't successful, what do you think happened?

- Could you approach it differently next time?

- What would you do when you negotiated again for the same thing?

- What would you not do…

"How does one become a butterfly?

You must want to fly so much, that you are willing to give up being a caterpillar."

- unknown

Lynda Hykin

THE LAST CHAPTER

THE NEW YOU!

If you are here, at this point in the book, you are fabulous! You are powerful! You are a new you! You have educated yourself. You have started down a new road... almost.

First you have to become aware of the old you and some things you might want to think about... changes you might want to make. Perhaps you realize you need to start doing some things, start doing some things differently, or even STOP doing some things. Let's check out how to make some positive changes that we now feel we need to make.

Perceptions and Habits

Definition of Insanity: "Doing the same thing over and over and expecting a different result" – Albert Einstein.

Habits live in our subconscious mind. They are defined as: The repetition of an act or thought repeated over and over until our subconscious mind reacts automatically. Did you know that our subconscious mind is 6 times more powerful than our conscious mind? It stores every thought we've ever had. It doesn't filter out **anything**. The more we repeat a thought or action, the bigger that file gets in our subconscious mind. Repeated often enough, we begin to automatically react to a certain situation seemingly without even thinking about it (consciously anyway). The more we repeat doing or thinking the same thing, the faster our subconscious mind can find 'the file' and send it up to our conscious mind. All our lives we've been doing this, creating habits.

We have developed our subconscious mind to work like this: This thought = this emotion = this reaction.

If we continue to live our life the way we always have, we will live our life the way we always have, purely out of habit.

When you wake up Monday morning, groggy, you reach into the cupboard, without even thinking about it for your coffee cup. It's there, you just know it's there. It's been in the same spot for years. However, on the weekend, you decided to rearrange your cupboards and moved the dishes around to make it easier to put them away. Now the cup is in a different cupboard. You are immediately taken out of your comfort zone. It doesn't feel right. Every morning for the next few days, you have to consciously remember where your coffee cup is. Eventually, reaching for your coffee cup in its new location will become the new habit. We have to create new habits that will replace the old. Our new-found freedom, our new life that we now choose to create will eventually live in a new comfort zone but you have to take that first step… and rearrange the cupboards.

It only takes 30 days to create a new habit, replacing the old one. Can you spend 30 days being uncomfortable to create a whole new life? Is your 'why' worth that? In order to become a butterfly, you must give up the comfort of being a caterpillar. Consciously practice going beyond your comfort zone and doing what scares you. Not just with negotiating and asking for what you want, but with everything in your life.

By expanding and stretching your comfort zone you will expand the size of your income. Right now, in this moment, if you are very comfortable with your life, and what you're doing, you are not growing. You are taking little or no risks. In order to grow, you have to get uncomfortable just for a little while. The next time you are feeling uncertain, or afraid about trying something new, doing something you've never done, instead of shrinking and retreating back to the safety of your comfort zone, move forward anyway.

If you continue in spite of the discomfort, in spite of what you feel, you will feel such a rush of empowerment! You will increase your self confidence immensely. Once that first time is conquered, the second time will be a little easier, and the third even more so. Eventually you will stretch further, attempt more and have more successes. The more no's you get, the more comfortable you get hearing them, and the less attached you become to them. Let them go. Treat every no like a success – because it is!

I treat my life like I'm in a slingshot. When fear, or something new comes into my life, I can feel myself resisting, resisting. Then when I just let go, the slingshot shoots my way up onto a whole new level. (Slingshots are usually always pointed UP). Whenever I feel that resistance, I'm now aware that I'm in a new place and push forward anyway.

A mistake is only a failure if you didn't learn from it. And a true failure is if you didn't even try.

Believe in yourself. Trust that you deserve to have whatever you want, that you are valuable, that you are worthy. You have earned the right to ask for what you want. And now you know how to do that! You are a negotiating machine!

Emotional Triggers

Unexpected events happen in life. When these certain events happen they set off certain triggers. You respond instinctively to events without thought. An trigger is something that activates your emotions instantly. It can be a rude name, a look one someone's face, a sarcastic remark, a violent movie, a crude joke or anything else you may react to negatively or positively. Something like these:

- For the smokers: When the phone rings, or you get in your car and turn on the ignition, you light up a cigarette – even if you just put one out. (As a former smoker, I know this one well!) The phone ringing is the trigger.
- Your children know which of your 'buttons' to push to get you to react; those 'buttons' are triggers. They can cause you to feel guilt, fear or anger.
- Happy triggers can cause you to smile, laugh or feel love

Triggers also occur in interviews:

- We have 2 other candidates that we are looking at –

  The trigger:

  - Competition; if I don't accept what they are offering, they will hire someone else.

  - Urgency; don't wait or the offer will be gone! This is one used over and over again in marketing campaigns, "One Day Only, buy NOW!!

- **The salary is $XXXXXX.00**

  The trigger is:

  - Final answer; this is what you will get, period. It's a closed statement that you believe requires a yes or no. You will either be excited or disappointed.
  - No control; You will get what we offer, take it or leave it

- **This position is part time but may lead to full time**
  o The trigger is:

  - The proverbial dangling of the carrot, or hope. The hope of becoming a permanent, full time employee which means job security, benefits, retirement plan.

- **We will make our decision next week**
- The trigger is:

  - Uncertainty – Do I wait? Accept the other company's offer? What if I wait, and then don't get the job?
  - Lack of control – You are at their mercy, you can't control the time or the decision

Learn to recognize your emotional triggers. Not just at work but at home, out in public, in a meeting, anywhere. If you can become aware of your emotional triggers, you can learn to catch yourself before you react, especially if your reaction is uncontrolled and detrimental to what you want.

When you suddenly feel upset, angry or guilty about something that just occurred:

- What was is it that caused your reaction?

- Can you determine why you reacted the way you did to that particular circumstance?

- How would it feel if you could find a way to react positively, or at the least neutrally?

Pet peeves are another form of trigger. Everyone has pet peeves. One of mine was pushy people; people that cut in line at a bus stop, or getting on a train. My reaction was always anger – "Hey! I was here first! That's not fair!" The result of this happening over and over again is – I became pushy! I began to assert my 'right' to that spot in line, by being just like them - pushy! Once I recognized it, I asked myself why it bothered me so much. It wasn't like I was being left behind. I didn't really miss out on anything. Did it really matter? Was it worth ruining my whole day, just because one person got in front of me?

I tried an experiment. For one week I decided that I was going to be last. Even if I was first in line, I would let other people go in front of me. What an amazing revelation! I began to feel good! It felt wonderful to let people go in front of me. And a funny thing happened. People started letting ME go in front of THEM! The emotion of anger was gone. It was replaced by joy. Who knew?

When you are negotiating, it may be emotional. Reaction to things said will happen automatically. But if you are prepared, if you are aware and recognize those triggers, you can avoid allowing the 'heat of the moment' to interfere. Even if it means you can't control the emotion, you will know that you need to take a break and remove yourself until the emotion is under control.

Empower yourself. Be aware of your triggers!

And finally …

Giving 110% is a great employee. Giving 200% without compensation is a schmuck. No-one benefits. Instead of loving your job, you begin to resent the extra hours and the time you have to take away from something else that is also important to you. Employees who are continually over-worked, start disengaging, 'sick' days start being used just to have a break. It is a lack of respect – both on the part of the boss or Company and on yourself. It leads to burn out, and a good chance that you will leave, for something not so demanding, or something more compensating.

When you see your work load starting to increase, become aware and start to track it. If it is a one time, huge opportunity, career making project and you are doing it with the expectation of a not-too-distance opportunity or reward, then make sure it is documented. Then make sure the boss knows you will be expecting a reward. When it is completed make sure you get that recognition. If it becomes ongoing, without the recognition, reward or compensation, then that's totally different. Do not let yourself be bullied or taken advantage of. When it starts to get out of control, take control and plan your negotiation strategy. Then take the initiative and do something about it. Don`t wait too long or you will lose the opportunity. Remember, habits over time become the norm. If you have been doing something for a long period of time, it has been silently agreed upon and it is now a normal part of your job.

Negotiating is not always about actual money. It doesn't always need a dollar value. Compensation can be as simple as recognition for a job well done. Sometimes I prefer that to money! Compliments and acknowledgement of your work make you want to do more. If only more employers realized this! We once got a rubber duck…yes, it's true! I thought it was hilarious! Yet it took a special place of honor in our tub. Just as a reminder for me, that I did something well and it was fun.

Would you ever want to set your bar so high, you lose a client? Can't see why would you ever do this? A very successful woman did not want to work with a certain client – she knew they would be 'high maintenance' and did not want to spend all her time working with them, because she knew they would never be happy and would continuously want more and more. They would eat up too much time at her current fee. When they asked what her fee was, she tripled her normal rate – and they accepted it without question! This was also the catalyst for her to greatly increase her fees from that point on, with little or no resistance! Even her current clients accepted an increase without issue or complaint. They knew the value they were getting.

Negotiating comes in many forms, and is done in many different ways for different reasons. It is simply a tool to help get the most out of your career and your life. You are here to experience the best life you can have, and asking for what you want will ensure you get it.

I hope this book has helped you in some way, given you insights, strategies and tools that you can use in your life, whether it's negotiating for money, a car, hotel accommodations, anything you want.

If there is only one thing to take away, I hope it is this: Always be true to you. Always act according to your core values. It's the inside that counts, how you feel when you are doing something. Don't ever compromise those values because they are what is special, what is unique about you. Learning to stand up for yourself, to ask for what you want, and to negotiate is one of the biggest steps you'll ever take. It is also one of the most empowering. But it will only be successful if it feels right.

Be you ... always.

My wish for you, and the purpose for writing this book, is to have women all over the world learn to negotiate, to understand the barriers and to break through those barriers, eliminating the wage gap, the inequality in opportunities for women, and empower women to make their own choices about what is best for them. It has been my privilege and pleasure to share this information with you. I now humbly ask that you go out and tell others, share this book, share the information and your experiences with others,

Lynda Hykin

both men and women, teenagers, College students, everyone.

With my deepest gratitude and appreciation, thank you.

A personal note from Lynda.

If you found some helpful information in this book, I would love for you to pass it on to someone else. It doesn't even have to be another woman. It could be a man, an enlightened leader who perhaps may understand women in the workplace a little more by reading this.

Buying them their own personal copy works great too!

Sharing information is how I learned so much over the last few years. It has helped me to grow. It has helped my bank account to grow.

I would also love to hear your story, so please email me and let me know about your successes and UN-successes. I take constructive criticism very well, so if there is any comment or information you would like to share with me, along with success stories I am always open and appreciate feedback.

I am living my dream – something I never thought would ever happen. In fact, this book is fulfilling a dream from when I was little – to be a writer. Please don't wait 50 years like I did!

You are not too old, too young, too set in your ways. Amazing things will happen the moment you decide you want a different life. I am living proof that it is possible.

And always remember:

The Genie WILL grant your wish – but you have to ask!

Always,

Lynda

Lynda Hykin

Diary of a Bald Lady

My Journey into the Land of Chrome Dom

– by Lynda Hykin

(Exclusive peek! The following is from my latest book that will be released in 2014)

Rude Reality, meet Madame Denial

April 14, 2013

Dear Diary,

I used to snicker at the men walking around with the really bad comb-over. I used to secretly laugh at the ones who had a bad toupe; it looked like a squirrel nesting on their head. Men with the horseshoe, or the part that was so low, it was almost at their jawline.

My Dad had the horseshoe, with a few strands desperately trying to cover up the large area of real estate on his head, unsuccessfully. For some reason it didn't look funny or weird on him. Except of course when the wind would get a hold of those precious few strands and stand them straight up, revealing to all what lay (or didn't lay) underneath. Kinda like the infamous picture of Marilyn Monroe, not so desperately trying to keep her dress down as it scandalously revealed her legs.

Donald Trump's do continues to amaze and confuse me. More so because he has millions of dollars that he could spend to make it look good, but he doesn't!

Some men embrace the bald, and shave it all off. I love these men! I find bald men incredibly sexy, I have ever since Telly Savalas.

Today, I no longer secretly laugh or snicker at those who are balding. Because at the age of 58, I have come out of the closet to declare that, I too am going bald.

The only difference between all those others and me is...

I am a woman.

I am a woman who is going bald.

I now have different questions about how I will wear my hair. A comb over? Go with the horseshoe? Plaster it down with mousse and gel and hairspray? Spend hours strategically placing every strand – only to have the wind stand it straight up revealing to all what doesn't lay underneath? (Pay backs are a bitch, aren't they?)

I have no idea why this is happening to me. I was born with very fine, thin hair. But is it genetics? Stress? One too many Toni Perms, because my Mom insisted I look like Shirley Temple? Perhaps it was the teasing, the backcombing, the cheap hair dye.

But no matter. When I wake up tomorrow, I will still be going bald.

I have seen beautiful bald women. Those beautiful courageous women that not only have to live with cancer, suffer through the torture of Chemo and radiation, but then also the loss of their hair. These women are truly beautiful. They should never have any doubts about it.

But I am not fighting such a battle. I am simply going bald. I see hair in the sink and I freak... and then I count them. Two more than yesterday! If I could, I would paste them back on my scalp.

About 2 years ago I noticed the thinning. I put it down to stress. Then I thought maybe it was the alcohol in the mousse. I blamed the hair gel – it was plugging up my head pores. (that's a technical term, I think)

My hairdresser suggested some shampoo that would open up any holes in my head that still had hair lying in wait underneath. I gladly shelled out $60 bucks to watch my seed (shampoo) sprouting little sprouts of hairlets.

I actually thought it started to grow back. Even my roommate asked if my hair was growing back. I was ecstatic.

Then, to help it along, I decided to let my natural color come out – and quit dyeing my hair. But the more grey my hair became, the more noticeable my scalp became. The two blended together so well, I REALLY started to look bald! I suffered through it, thinking all the while that once all the other color was gone, it would be better.

I also went into my first 'wig store' and tried on grey wigs, to get the feel of the look. Of course these wigs had tons of hair on them! I couldn't relate, not only to the grey color but the thickness of the hair! It was like a 20 lb weight on my head. But I continued to let the grey grow.

I am a Speaker and Trainer a somewhat public figure. I thought it was time to be me. It would also be much easier for photo shoots. Grey is grey. I wouldn't be light brown one month, and reddy brown the next. I wouldn't confuse my audience. They would now always recognize me – the lady with the grey hair. I convinced myself that it would make me more credible, more authentic, more wise. I was one hair cut away from being completely grey, when I chickened out. I couldn't handle it.

The darker hair color definitely made it appear like I had more hair says Madame Denial. This kept me satisfied until just recently. I decided I really wanted to let the grey come out. I was tired of being a different shade every time I colored my hair, it was like a surprise in every box. Reddish brown, brownish red, oops, very red. Almost black, should've been brown but went black, golden browny yellow. It was different every time. The ones that I really liked I said I would remember the number, sometimes I even kept the number off the box. But whenever I once again decided to get a color for my hair, I never had the number with me.

Then tragedy struck. Which gave birth to this blog. I wanted to once again let the grey grow. After a trip that sun bleached my hair (the color really looked good btw) the roots started up – grey. I got 3 weeks into it and noticed how much my scalp was showing so early this time. I freaked and ran to the store and got #50, dark brown. Applied. Waited the allotted time (okay, that's a lie. The box said 25 minutes – I have never left hair dye on for more than 20 and refused to this time). Blow dry. Look in the mirror. Whoa, kinda dark. But okay. Wait a minute. What's that? OMG! I can STILL see my scalp! I yanked the hair apart to check the roots. Yep, they were dark (not as dark as the rest – never is). I took a look a my part. It looked like my head was parting like The Red Sea! A thousand people could have trekked through there without trampling a single strand! With shaking hands I performed the ultimate test. At the Front of my head, where bangs normally commence, I pulled the hair straight up. And I could see right through to the back! I could, if I wasn't so messed up, have probably counted what now was left.

I was stunned. The hair dye would no longer lie about what was happening. Everyone would know. I could no longer deceive anyone – or myself. I was going bald. The horse was gone, the barn door was closed. There was no turning back.

What to do, what to do?

Rude Reality became a hair stalker. I checked out old ladies, young girls, professional women, women hanging out on the street corner. On the bus, at events, sitting in the mall. Some had more, some had less. None of them looked like they cared! But I did! I DON'T WANT TO BE BALD!!

Tragedy to triumph, I'm always looking for ways to turn challenges in my life into strengths. Hey! "I could talk about this to other women" was one thought followed immediately by this second thought: "Hi, my name is Lynda and I'm bald." Now if you heard someone say that, what would you do? Don't lie, you would do one of three things:

a) stare at my glowing dome

b) try NOT to stare at my glowing dome

c) Check out my head to see if I'm wearing a wig

and four: Subconsciously touch your own hair to make sure it's still there!

Whatever profound presentation I may have, it would be lost because they would be looking, not listening.

So, I could not see myself standing on stage and talking about it.

My next thought was – get a wig. A really cool wig. I could maybe pull a Dolly Parton and have a closet full of wigs. I could have fun with this! Every day a different wig! Play dress up! BUT...

I still have some hair left. Madame Denial reminded me that the comb-overs and mousse and hairspray and hours of strategically placing each strand is still working. And if I start wearing a wig, it will make what I have left fall out faster. Then I WILL be truly bald. 'They' say if you wear hats, you will go bald, if you wear wigs you will go bald. I'm still not ready to voluntarily kill what little is left!

I wondered how many other women are out there suffering with this?

Because you attract what you think about, I am starting to see women everywhere in my community with thinning hair. Maybe it's this toxic city! Come to think of it, when I was in Vancouver, my hair was still on my head, and not in my sink. Healthy eating, fresh air, exercise – could that help? Is it too late? Inquiring minds want to know. Where do I go?

Do they have hair plugs for women? How many plugs do I need? Does that laser stuff that they show on the late, late, late, really late show work?

Can I take supplements to help? HELP!!

And so the birth of the blog. Trying to come up with catchy little names to get peoples attention – BMW – bald men and women. Nope. Want this to be just for women. The bald blog – simple, but email was taken. The Bald and the Beautiful – taken. Then I came up with Girls gone bald. Great! email available, no website with that name. Would people remember it? Should. Would they know what it's about? Should – oh crap. Wait a minute. Better rethink this one.

- How about Headless honeys? Nope – a little too S & M.

- Women going bald. Yawn.

- Hair loss for women, sounds like I'm trying to GET them to go bald.

- Thin hair in thirty days. Hmmm, possible.

- Shit! I'm bald. (Probably get kicked off WordPress for that one.)

- Little Bo Dare, has lost her hair... ya no, again, I'm seeing freaky thinking here.

This is harder than it looks! I want a respectful, serious yet playful name.

Something that people won't mind talking about and sharing with others. After all, that's the whole point of this blog. Okay look up the medical term for this. Maybe the name of this would be a cool blog name. (NOT!)

Medical Name: Androgenic alopecia. Ya, that's not happening. I can't even pronounce it! "I have a blog about baldnesss." Oh really, what's it called? Um, can't pronounce it but it's about going bald. Nope. But it did make me think of the childhood French song - **singing to the tune of Aloutte**

Alopecia, gentille Alopecia
Alopecia, je te plumerai
Je te plumerai la tête
Je te plumerai la tête
Et la tête, et la tête
Alopecia, Alopecia
O-o-o-o-oh
Alopecia, gentille Alopecia
Alopecia, je te plumerai

(Bet you got that running around in your head right now, don't you! … You're welcome!) A little excerpt and definition of AA here – not to be confused with the other AA:

The majority of women with androgenic alopecia have diffuse thinning on all areas of the scalp. Men on the other hand, rarely have diffuse thinning but instead have more distinct patterns of baldness. Some women may have a combination of two pattern types. Androgenic alopecia in women is due to the action of androgens, male hormones that are typically present in only small amounts. Androgenic alopecia can be caused by a variety of factors tied to the actions of hormones, including, ovarian cysts, the taking of high androgen index birth control pills, pregnancy, and menopause. Just like in men the hormone DHT appears to be at least partially to blame for the miniaturization of hair follicles in women suffering with female pattern baldness. Heredity plays a major factor in the disease.

Wow, how hard can this be! I'd put my thinking cap on, but as I stated before, hats for balding people are no-no's. After they're bald, they're good to go!

FINALLY! April 14th, I finally found the perfect name: Diary of a Bald Lady. Website available? Check. Email address available? Check.

I can't believe I'm excited about writing about baldness – my baldness!! (I can hear the trampling of the therapists now, racing to my door step!)

I even created names for the two 'people' hanging out in my brain. So, meet Rude Reality and Madame Denial. So much more fun to write about them than me. From time to time, I will be blogging about their conversations, arguments, and I'm sure mutual crying jags together. (Again with the therapists and they have me on speed dial!)

And so I begin on this 'unique' journey. If you are a comrade in arms, hold your hairbrush filled with deserters high and come out of the closet. Come with me as I journey into the unknown land of Chrome Dome.

Always,
Lynda

As you can tell from the above, since writing 'Negotiation for Women' my life has taken a very unique turn. I have two choices – run and hide or follow this new journey and see where it leads. I choose the second. You can follow my blog at www.diaryofabaldlady.com

The book will be a one year journey, so please look for it next Spring.

WHAT'S NEW AND EXCITING
for Negotiation for Women!

This book will soon be available in Audio format – a 3 CD collection.

Check on the website www.negotiationforwomen.com for details and availability.

Fun and enlightening booklet!

"100 Ways to become UN-Successful; The Only Guide to being Broke and UN-happy" is a promotional booklet available through Kindle, PDF or hard copy for only $4.97

It is a humorous yet enlightening take on what NOT to do with your money. In this booklet, I am the "What NOT to do Guru" having done all the wrong things with my money over and over again.

$2 from every sale of the hard copy goes toward Because I am a Girl Organization.

I have also added a 1 hour keynote presentation and a 3 Hour Seminar for Teens called, "What do you do with a Dollar?". They are available free to high schools in Canada and the US. (some conditions apply – please email for details)

Lynda Hykin

ABOUT THE AUTHOR

Lynda Hykin is The Money Match-Maker

"Matching women with their money through the power of Negotiation"

Lynda is a recognized voice whose topics include issues of wage inequality, gender differences in the workplace, and women and leadership. Using her research findings and drawing on vast personal experience, this engaging, highly credible woman leaves her audience with enlightening and actionable ideas and insights for improving their money, their career and their life.

Lynda addresses audiences from Professional Companies and Organizations, Colleges and Universities, Administrative and Women's Groups, and Non-Profit Organizations throughout Canada and the USA with the vision of sharing her message globally. She also speaks to high schools and Youth Organizations.

She is also the author of 100 Ways to Be UN-Successful – the Only Guide to being Broke and UN-Happy. A self proclaimed Guru of what NOT to do having done all the wrong things with her money, this is an enlightening and 'tongue in cheek' look at what NOT to do with your money.

To check for availability to book for a Keynote Speaking engagement or for a seminar, contact negotiationforwomen@gmail.com

The website www.negotiatonforwomen.com will also have postings of events held by Lynda, so please check it out!

Lynda Hykin

RESOURCES

Excerpt from 2013 Rosenzweig Report:

Quote: The latest *Rosenzweig Report on Women at the Top Levels of Corporate Canada* finds 8 percent of the highest paying executive positions are held by women, almost double the 4.6 percent in the first Rosenzweig survey commissioned eight years ago.

"On the eve of International Women's Day, we release our 8th annual Rosenzweig Report with guarded optimism," says Jay Rosenzweig, Managing Partner of Rosenzweig & Company. "Guarded because the corporate world is still largely dominated by men; but optimistic because there is a trajectory of positive change. We choose to believe that the glass is half full and the tipping point is near."

Leslie O'Donoghue, who is on the list as Executive Vice President, Corporate Development & Strategy and Chief Risk Officer of Calgary-based Agrium Inc. (TSX and NYSE: AGU), says this year's Rosenzweig Report clearly indicates a positive trend.

"These results and upward trend are encouraging," says Ms O'Donoghue. "The more women achieve a presence in the boardroom and within the executive ranks, the more their value and contribution will be recognized in the corporate workplace, paving the path for other women to succeed."

Rosenzweig said women leaders at large Canadian companies are still the exception, not the rule - as they are in most of the world - but the upward trend is encouraging.

"Are there still obstacles in front of women as they vie for top leadership roles?" Mr. Rosenzweig asks. "Perhaps, but there are clear signs that things are changing; from shareholders, boards of directors and governments encouraging change; to women themselves asserting their talents and making it known that they want these top jobs. Half of Canada's provincial premiers are now women and they're governing 87% of the population.

We're seeing female leaders emerge everywhere and the corporate world will be no different."

For full Report visit
http://rosenzweigco.com/mediacenter/diversity/index.html

More Resources

- The "Women's Economic Opportunity Index"

- Statistics Canada

- Catalyst

Books that are a must to Read:

- "Ask For It" - Linda Babcock and Sarah Levescher *(This book started my quest to learn more!)*

- "Secrets of Six Figure Women" – Barbara Stanny *(One of my **favorite** 'virtual' mentors!)*

- "Overcoming Under-Earning" – Barbara Stanny

- "The Good Girls Guide to Negotiating" - Leslie Whitaker and Elizabeth Austin

- "Impact!" – Nancy Solomon

- "Secrets of the Millionaire Mind" – T. Harv Eker *(This started my financial freedom journey!)*

- "The Passion Test" – Chris and Janet Atwood

- "Making the Impossible Possible" – Bill Strickland

Lynda Hykin

101 Wise Women of the World Society

I am truly blessed and grateful to have the thought, the dream, the audacity to believe I can fulfill my passion by following the most daunting, inspiring and unimaginable journeys I have ever been on. I share it with you here.

Programs

Pearls of Wisdom

Connecting women at all levels of leadership development and skills development with unparalleled exposure to people, places, opportunities, mentorship, skills and ideas that will make their Community a World Class Community.

Pearls of Hope

To transform the lives of homeless, pregnant women and their children by identifying and overcoming the root causes of homelessness, and by promoting physical and emotional health, spiritual growth and financial independence.

Pearls of Potential

Uncovering and bringing to light the awareness of a person's true passion and purpose through exposure to various educational environments for adults-in-transition as well as at-risk youth.

At the time of Publication, this Non-profit Organization is still in The Dreaming Room. If you would like more information or would like to become involved in this dynamic and impactful global journey, please contact me @ 101wisewomen@gmail.com

Lynda Hykin

www.ingramcontent.com/pod-product-compliance
Lightning Source LLC
Chambersburg PA
CBHW030928180526
45163CB00002B/500